P9-CCM-637

It's a Wonderful (Mid)life!

IT'S A WONDERFUL (Mid) LIFE!

Finding the Positives in Aging

Sheila Rabe

HORIZON BOOKS

A DIVISION OF CHRISTIAN PUBLICATIONS, INC.
CAMP HILL, PENNSYLVANIA

Horizon Books
A Division of Christian Publications, Inc.
3825 Hartzdale Drive, Camp Hill, PA 17011
www.cpi-horizon.com

ISBN: 0-88965-162-0
© 1999 by Horizon Books
All rights reserved
Printed in the United States of America

99   00   01   02   03   5   4   3   2   1

Cover photo by Linda Wolf,
Bainbridge Island, Washington

Unless otherwise indicated,
Scripture taken from the HOLY BIBLE:
NEW INTERNATIONAL VERSION ®.
Copyright © 1973, 1978, 1984 by the
International Bible Society. Used by
permission of Zondervan Bible Publishers.

Scripture references labeled "KJV"
are taken from the
Holy Bible: King James Version.

Scripture references labeled "RSV"
are taken from the
New Revised Standard Version Bible,
copyright, 1989, by the
Division of Christian Education of the National Council
of the Church of Christ in the U.S.A.
Used by permission. All rights reserved.

Scripture references labeled "TLB"
are taken from The Living Bible.
Copyright © 1971 by Tyndale House Publishers.
All rights reserved.

Contents

Acknowledgments

Thank you very much!

BECAUSE MIDDLE-AGED WOMEN in America are such a kaleidoscope of experiences, writing about the experiences of just one wouldn't be nearly so helpful as dishing out collective advice. So before I started this book I took a survey. There were no control groups, no blinds, no statistics—just a small sampling of women around the country who gave me their opinions on a variety of midlife topics. Some participated anonymously. Some signed their names and gave me permission to quote them, which I do from time to time throughout this book.

To all those women I say, "Thank you. Your advice was often profound, your humor encouraging, and I couldn't have done this book without you. God bless you all!"

Introduction

And Then Came Forty

 AGING IS A FUNNY THING. (I keep telling myself that!) You don't notice it in the early stages. When I was a little girl I lived for birthdays. They meant cake and ice cream, games and balloons, running, screaming and laughing. (Come to think of it, my birthdays are still like that. It's just that none of us can run as fast or as far as we could a few years ago.) I rushed through my twenties, unaware of the quickly passing years. It wasn't until thirty that it dawned on me that my body hadn't come with a lifetime warranty. Then came forty—and industrial strength depression. I'd just gotten it together and now it was falling apart.

Things were beginning to sag. My lipstick was starting to bleed. Store clerks called me "Ma'am."

And I wasn't the only one aging. My parents, whom I'd assumed would be around almost forever, were crumbling before my very eyes. My children weren't as big as I was—they were bigger. And they were trying their best to complete the silver dye job nature had begun on my hair. Suddenly I realized I'd hit middle age.

Middle age! For me, those two words conjured up images from a popular newspaper cartoon I used to read when I was young, called "The Girls." It featured plump little ladies in orthopedic shoes who always managed to make themselves look ridiculous. That wasn't me. Was it?

And that nasty image of a woman's middle years was only part of the problem. Now, at the ripe old age of ___ (you didn't *really* think I was going to tell, did you?), I've realized that I've used up the first half of my life. That leaves only one half for all that God has given me to do.

Ever notice that when your car's gas gauge falls to half, how quickly it runs down to empty? Well, if life is like a gas tank—gulp!

We all cope with different aging issues. For those who are vain, it's the loss of our looks; for those whose identity has been as a mother, it's the loss of our babies. Those who have juggled a career and family may want to drop both and limp away to a health spa. Many face health issues, problems with reentering the job market or having to deal with suddenly dependent parents. Some see our few remaining earning years and worry about how we'll keep our financial boat afloat after retirement. Others may find themselves suddenly single after many years of marriage, feeling abandoned. Still others who have never married face a society that says, "Well, why not? What's wrong with you?" Probably all of us have to cope with more than one of these issues at once.

Sometimes we simply don't realize the wonder of our lives. We see the frustrations and irritations instead of the goals achieved and lives touched. We see negatives instead of positives and past mistakes instead of future possibilities. By looking in all the wrong places, we miss what's right in front of us—the evidence that God is so very good to those who love Him. For all of us, His word holds the answers, the comfort and the encouragement we need.

After searching His Word and seeing my life through His eyes, I've reached a conclusion: even though I'm already in support hose with orthopedic shoes following close behind, I can still have a wonderful midlife. And so, I hope, can you.

I hope this book will answer at least some of your burning midlife questions. I know that writing it has answered many of mine.

Chapter 1

What Do My Skin and Old Underwear Have in Common?

"Youth and beauty, man. That's the ticket."
   Elise Elliot, *First Wives Club*
"Baloney."
   Sheila Rabe, First (and last) wife

WELL, NOW, DON'T I sound like I've got it all together? Actually, it's all falling apart, and that was my problem for a long time. I had discovered the middle age version of "Happy Birthday":

Happy birthday to me.
New wrinkles I see,
and everything's sagging.
Happy birthday to me.

I first noticed the change when I was sitting at my computer. I just happened to look down at the keyboard. There they were: Grandma's hands, complete with raised blue veins, age spots and skin like you see on wrinkled dogs. How had my grandmother's hands gotten on the ends of my arms?

Don't get me wrong. I loved my grandmother. I just never planned on looking like her. In fact, I never planned on looking like any of the older women who paraded through my life as a child, even though I thought they were all fascinating—in a three-legged dog sort of way.

There was Edith, Mom's beautician. She wore Bride-of-Frankenstein hair and THE EYEBROWS, thickly penciled in so that everyone would see them. (Mom took me to Edith to get my hair done once. I left with hair standing higher than the Eiffel tower and sprayed until it was just as sturdy.)

Then there was Frannie, my mom's pretty friend with the shiny skin under her eyes. I used to wonder what made her skin look like that. Then I tried cold cream to kill the wrinkles under my eyes and got the same Mop 'n Glow™ shine.

And good old Miss Prym. We've all seen her. I remember thinking how the bright circles of red on her wrinkled cheeks made her look like Raggedy Ann. It wasn't long ago that I was a little too free with the blush myself and looked like good old Miss Prym.

But getting back to my skin. It fell prey to Old Underwear Syndrome. With new underwear you can pull on the waistband and the energetic elastic snaps tightly into place as soon as you let go. Old underwear just hangs, limp and lifeless. These days, so does my skin.

Skin isn't the only problem. Middle age spread really exists. I'm living proof. If my chest gets any bigger, I'll

be a natural for one of those Valkyries in a Wagner op-
era—the ones with Viking horns and glass-shattering
voices. And I have no waist anymore. I look like a tree
trunk.

An old friend got skinny taking Chinese herbs, so I or-
dered some. They made me feel like I had the flu. Not only
that—they got me so buzzed I'd be up at 4 a.m. writing letters to everyone I knew, including the mail lady. (With all
these letters, we were getting to be good buddies.) My
friend, the doctor's wife, told me the stuff would give me a
stroke and trash my kidneys. My sister-in-law informed me
that she wouldn't come see me when I was in the hospital
getting dialysis. I concluded that being lithe and slim
wouldn't do me any good as a corpse, so I bagged the herbs.

Which brought me back to being a middle-aged
woman. My body is never going to be twenty again—no
matter how much I lie about my age. (Denial won't
change reality any more than Chinese herbs.)

Why was I acting like this? Could it be because I come
from a long line of vain females? I remember the day my
mother announced that she'd discovered a new wrinkle
on her face.

"Mom," I said, "you're eighty-three. Why are you surprised?" What I didn't say was, "You already have so
many, how could you possibly notice a new one?"

The reality check didn't help. My mom bemoaned the
fact that her skin just wasn't what it had once been—"Just
like peaches and cream," my dad used to say. It was a funny
thing about my dad. Even in their seventies, he still thought
my mother was the most beautiful woman in the world.

And I thought she was still pretty cute at eighty-three.
Yes, she was a little old lady, but she was such a cute one.

"Mom, I think you look fine," I said. And I meant it. When I looked at my mother I saw with eyes of love the woman who filled the afternoons of my childhood with the aroma of baking cookies, the woman who laughed a lot, who sang slightly off-key harmonies to my father's melodies, and who was the most infinitely fascinating person in my entire young life. This was the woman who spent hours curling my hair, who played double solitaire with me as a teenager and who lovingly helped plan every detail of my wedding. Whoever said "Pretty is as pretty does" knew my mother.

So if I could so easily see my mother's silliness, why couldn't I see it in myself? Why did I obsess over new wrinkles around my eyes, pull the skin at my temples and wish my skin would stay that way? Somewhere along the way, I had bought our culture's phony line that the young and beautiful have the highest worth.

Save back issues of your favorite magazine for a year. Spread them out. Now, try to find an issue that doesn't have an article about how to trim your thighs, hide your flaws or look younger in ten minutes a day.

I randomly browsed through a stack of women's magazines. They represented most major secular women's magazines, and the cover of every one promised at least one article on how to improve my looks.

An issue of *Redbook* promised: "ERASE WRINKLES –The New Ten Minute Facial Peel."[1] (Peel away my wrinkles in ten minutes? Sign me up!) *Ladies' Home Journal* cried: "HOW MODELS DO IT—Easy Ways to Look Younger."[2] *Good Housekeeping* gave me "ONE-MINUTE MAKEOVERS, LOOK PRETTIER NOW."[3] And an old *Family Circle* promised

"MAKEUP MAGIC—YOUR BIGGEST PROBLEMS SOLVED."[4] (Imagine that. My biggest problems solved with makeup.)

In America, the cosmetics business is big business. When I last checked, we were buying $2.48 billion worth of goodies annually to make us beautiful.[5] I'm sure that figure has increased since then.

There's hardly a model or actress who isn't peddling a fitness video. And maybe that's good for them, because great roles for actresses usually disappear with age. Actresses aren't the only ones who have a tough time proving themselves after middle age. After forty, its hard for any woman to find a job.

My friend, Grandma Gorgeous, is in her late forties and currently unemployed. She's an energetic woman who certainly doesn't look or act like a grandmother. But the person at the employment agency said her age was working against her.

Why? I ask. Women in their forties and fifties should be in demand. Our children are raised. We don't take pregnancy leaves, and we don't miss work because Junior has the chicken pox. We don't wear racy outfits that distract male coworkers, and we have the kind of common sense acquired from years of experience.

A middle-aged woman is a great asset! So why would anyone, when deciding between a twenty-two-year-old and a forty-two-year-old not pick the older woman (other than the fact that the sweet young thing will probably work for less)? Maybe for the same reason rising businessmen replace their first mate with young "trophy wives." In our society, youth is a prize to be captured and held. Youth and beauty are synonymous.

But beauty is more than tight skin and a barely-broken-in body. Beauty is ageless. We aging baby boomers prove that. So many women are breaking the middle-age stereotype—choosing fit and well-dressed over flabby and frumpy. We don't look or act as our mothers did at our age. If we have crow's feet around our eyes, so what? A few wrinkles won't make a smile lit by a sweet spirit any less warm. Beauty really is in the eyes of the beholder. Those who love us will think we're beautiful no matter what our age.

Our culture's obsession with physical appearance is off-base, but there's nothing wrong with enjoying beauty. God, our Creator, decorated our entire planet with beautiful plants, trees, mountains and lakes. He scattered stars like jewels across the universe for His and our enjoyment. And speaking of beauty, I'll bet Adam and Eve would have put Mr. and Miss Universe to shame. But judging worth simply by appearance can be dangerous. Genesis 3:6 gives a good example of that.

Satan has convinced Eve that up is down and down is up. She looks at the forbidden tree and sees that it pleases the eye. *Well*, she reasons, *something so beautiful must be worth investigating.* We all know how her investigation turned out.

Ever wonder about Esther, winner of history's first recorded beauty contest? Her beauty won her first place in King Xerxes' heart, and he made Esther his queen. But then her entire race faced extermination from that same king. Her cousin and advisor, Mordecai, pointed out that beauty wouldn't save her from suffering the same fate as the rest of the Jews. He suggested that, perhaps, her great beauty was God's tool to get her to the throne.

There, she could have the influence and opportunity to save His people (Esther 4:13-14).

Esther did the right thing. She acted bravely and saved her people. To this day, the Jewish feast of Purim celebrates her bravery. What place would Esther have in history if she had been only a pretty face?

The story of Jacob makes a good object lesson for those of us inclined to worship beauty. We first meet Jacob in Genesis 25. Old sneaky Jacob, out to get those good things his unrighteous brother, Esau, scorned. Jacob knew something valuable when he saw it, which is why he tricked Esau out of the family inheritance. But Jacob wasn't so astute in picking a wife. Have you ever taken part in a white elephant gift exchange? When you picked the most beautifully wrapped gift—only to get the biggest dud under the tree? That is what happened to Jacob. He fell in love with the packaging and didn't stop to think about what was inside.

The Bible tells us that Jacob's choice, Rachel, was lovely. But her poor sister, Leah, had weak eyes. Maybe that meant Leah couldn't see well and squinted a lot. Or perhaps her eyes were less vibrantly colored than Rachel's. No one knows for sure. We do know that Rachel was the local beauty queen while Leah had to settle for Miss Congeniality.

Jacob met Rachel when he returned to his father's homeland to visit his Uncle Laban. It wasn't long before he struck a deal. "Uncle Laban, let me marry your daughter, Rachel, and I'll work for you gratis for seven years," Jacob said. Most of us know the story. Come the wedding night, Uncle Laban swathed Leah in wedding veils and finery. He pulled a switch, and Jacob the deceiver got a taste of his own medicine.

I think it is fascinating how God put yet another twist on Laban's trick. Jacob wanted Rachel, the beauty. But when he got Leah, Jacob really got the nicer of the two sisters. We see Leah, quietly loving Jacob, hoping desperately with each new baby that maybe now he will return her love. After Judah's birth, Leah's focus changes from her husband to God. She says, "This time I will praise the Lord."

It's a good thing Leah turned to God, because Jacob's heart still belonged to beautiful, spoiled Rachel. Rachel turned childbearing into such a contest that it reduced Leah to bargaining for Jacob's attention. Rachel said, "Give me children or I'll die." Ironically, Rachel eventually died in childbirth. With her last breath, she tried to leave the child a legacy of guilt by naming him Ben-Oni, Son of my Trouble. (Fortunately for Benjamin, his father changed his name to Son of My Right Hand.)

Rachel caused other problems on the home front. She also stole the family idol from her father when Jacob wanted to return to his homeland. She knew that when daddy died, the child who possessed this family image inherited the estate. When Laban came after them, Rachel concealed her theft by plunking herself down on the saddlebag containing the stolen image. "Sorry I can't get up to greet you properly, Daddy," she said. "I'm having my period." In the account of her life, we see no indication that Rachel ever shifted her focus to God. From beginning to end, she focused only on herself.

For Leah, the story ends better than it begins. Somewhere along the way, her husband came to appreciate her.

When Jacob lay dying, he didn't ask to be buried with Rachel. Poor, unloved Leah had the honor of burial with Jacob's family. I like to think Jacob finally saw the beauty below the surface and came to regard Leah as the gem she was.[6]

Jacob wasn't the only man in Bible history to fall for a pretty face. Samson fell hard for Delilah. David coveted Bathsheba. In each case the man made his choice based purely on physical beauty—and lived to regret it.

When we worship beauty, we give our hearts to a false god. Proverbs 31:30 says, "Beauty is fleeting." Why work so hard to serve a master that won't be around for long?

Even after we've worked hard on our looks, how many of us really feel beautiful? I have yet to meet a woman who is happy with her body. We can always find something to complain about: big breasts, small breasts; big thighs, small calves; curly hair, straight hair; fine hair, coarse hair; big feet, big nose, big hips, bad skin. I've heard those complaints and more. And I've said half of them!

Aging is more than a fact of life. It is the result of sin. God told Adam, "Dust you are and to dust you will return" (Genesis 3:19). But there is good news. Although we may be crumbling outwardly, we are continually being changed, made new and improved (2 Corinthians 4:16), by the power of God. A time will come when we exchange our worn-out bodies for something much better (1 Corinthians 15:53-56). That sounds good to me. If given a choice between new appliances and fixing up the old ones, which would you take?

Peter said, "Your beauty should not come from outward adornment, such as braided hair and the wearing of gold jewelry and fine clothes. Instead, it should be that of your inner self, the unfading beauty of a gentle and quiet spirit, which is of great worth in God's sight" (I Peter 3:3-4). When I was young I just didn't get what he meant. But now that I'm older, I'm beginning to see.

In fact, I saw very clearly one day at a youth gathering. Three teenage girls sat on a couch. Two of them were what my son would call "babes." Complete with lipstick and the latest jewelry style—a million rings on each hand—they were gorgeous. The third girl had lovely eyes and a beautiful complexion, but by the world's standards, she was a Leah compared to the other two. Yet, Leah Junior looked superior. Her sweetness glowed like a halo. It made the other two, who definitely lacked in the sweetness department, look like cheap imitations.

Maybe two out of three women recommend striving for beauty. But it's the remaining one who doesn't panic when the ribbons start fraying. She survives the crumbling of her body with her spirits up (we know everything else is going to droop!) and her self-image intact.

Our culture says beauty leads to acceptance. It doesn't tell us that because it is true, but because it supports our economy. The diet industry, the fitness biz (videos, exercise equipment, health clubs), the cosmetics and fashion industries—think of all the businesses that would suffer if women said, "Hey, the way I look is just fine." Maybe I owe it to my country to keep dying my hair!

But I don't owe it to my friends to reinforce that cultural message. We mean comments like "You are *so* pretty" or "I wish I had your figure" to flatter—and they do. But they don't encourage our friends to focus on what God considers most important: character. There is nothing wrong with saying, "What a pretty dress!" or "You sure look nice today." But every time we act as if *they* are somehow responsible for the way they've been put together, we are setting them up for trouble. If we only affirm their looks, how will they feel when those looks start to fade?

With her long, blond hair, hazel eyes, perfect features and tanned body, Lovely Louise stops hearts. Whenever she walks into a room, male heads swivel. But approaching forty was painful. Reality stepped in and said, "Hey, baby, your days on center stage are numbered." Fortunately, Louise had invested in more than her looks. She'd developed friendships and sports skills. To help get past a landmark birthday, she celebrated with *several* parties and soon saw that forty, like fifty or sixty, is just a number. She has sailed into her forties with self-esteem intact—no thanks to society.

Dr. Anthony Campolo says that by overemphasizing attractiveness in women, society helps us feel like failures when the passage of time erodes.[7] (Gee, guys, thanks for the help!) But as Christians, we don't listen to society. We listen to God. And in the same verse that talks about how fleeting beauty is (Proverbs 31:30), He gives us the real definition of success: "a woman who fears the LORD is to be praised." Does anyone remember Miss America of 1975? Does anyone care? How about Mother Teresa? Anyone know her?

Let's stop reinforcing the wrong beliefs society has forced on us. Instead of complimenting little Suzie's pretty curls, I can compliment the lovely dress that her mother made. Better yet, I'll compliment her good behavior or special achievements. Talents and good deeds can be cultivated and used to build up the body of Christ. Those are things for which we can take responsibility and which we can legitimately pursue.

After several years of singing the birthday blues, I realized I was hitting some sour notes. I took another look at the growing number of candles on my cake, and this is what I found:

Christian Women Can Only Improve with Age

Paul says in Second Corinthians 3:18 that we are continually being changed into the Lord's likeness. The longer God has to work with us, the better we get.

Writer Pat Rushford is living proof of this. When I first met Pat, she was in her forties and had several impressive nonfiction books to her credit, like *What Kids Want Most in a Mom*. I liked her immediately. Now Pat is in her fifties, and she has two best-selling mystery series. Her skin doesn't cling as tightly to her neck anymore. Her hips have widened. But she still has beautiful eyes, a keen mind and a wonderful sense of humor. When I attend my favorite yearly writers' conference, seeing her is one of the highlights.

Pat's philosophy on aging is simple: There is no sense putting out energy to fight something you can't stop. Pat says that the key is to accept the fact that you're aging. "Once you're able to face your own death, it pushes you to a different dimension," she says. "You're able to not worry about it."

"It's not my death I'm having a hard time facing," I insisted when she shared her philosophy. "It's the loss of my looks, my youth."

But Pat (who also happens to have a master's degree in psychology) reminded me that it's normal to grieve when we lose something—whether a loved one, a job or our youth. "But then," says Pat, "you realize you're gaining something: wisdom. The older I get, the closer I get to God." This brings me to another benefit of aging ...

New Birthdays Equal New Opportunities

Our young and attractive years are also the most fertile; we are at our reproductive peak. All those active female hormones inspire equally active male hormones and, voila! We get a mate and, usually, some offspring. Aging is what moves women from the childbearing and child rearing stage of life, which lasts only for a season.

Then we move on to communal support activities such as helping younger women with their children (our society calls this grandmothering), church involvement, aid for the needy, personal growth and other larger-based activities. If we never grew past the attract-a-mate stage, we would be lifelong baby machines. Wrinkles do not signal THE END, just the end of a phase—and the beginning of another.

Each new year of life brings new friends, new responsibilities, new chances to learn and grow, new opportunities for God to use me. Who knows what person I may impact in this next year of my life? Who knows what new challenges await me? I am the heroine in an adventure series, and another story begins with each birthday.

With Age Comes Wisdom

In *Modern Maturity*, columnist Judith Martin (also known as Miss Manners), said that trying to pretend we're young when we're not "deprives age of its great dignity and advantage."[8] She said when she was young, she longed to be older. Her father said, "I can just see you some day wearing high-collared blouses, holding a stick, tyrannizing generations of your descendants." And Miss Manners thought, "Yes, that's what I'm after. I was really born for this role."

I don't see myself shaking a stick and tyrannizing my grandkids, but I do see that old age is like a hard-earned merit badge. You earn it after surviving emotional wounds and triumphing over hard times. I have heard many women say, "I'm proud of these gray hairs. I earned every one of them." They've got a point.

The book of Proverbs says, "The glory of young men is their strength, gray hair the splendor of the old" (20:29). Youth enjoys power and energy, but, like my friend Pat said, with age comes wisdom. I am a walking encyclopedia of life experiences with information on everything from how to cope with a colicky baby to how to handle sticky social situations. I have been in the school of life for a long time and have graduated to the status of—if not grand master—at least master. And Miss Manners is right. That involves a certain level of dignity that just can't be conferred on the young. In fact, according to the Bible, we who are more mature should "train the younger women to love their husbands and children, to be self-controlled and pure, to be busy at home, to be kind, and to be subject to their husbands" (Titus 2:4-5). Younger women should look to us as role models. This means that instead of trying to look like them, we need to model positive behavior for them.

You may be thinking, *That's great for you, Sheila, but I still want a tummy tuck and a facelift.* Been there, thought that. A friend loaned me a great book, *Beauty and the Best.* In this book, the author listed plastic surgery's many draw-backs. I learned that Mr. Doctor could have an "oops moment" that could leave me with a snipped nerve and permanent droop on my face. Or I could suffer cardiac arrest and die on the operating table. At the very least, I would experience bruising and great pain, and my bank account would go into shock.

Still, I remember thinking, *I don't care. I want a facelift and a nose job.* And that was when I had my vision—a real, live, Old Testament prophet-style vision. The thing rolled in my mind as if I were watching a movie.

In this vision I had my new face, and the lovely, young, perfect-nosed me was flying up to heaven. The trip was quick, and before I could say "young and beautiful" I stood in front of enormous golden gates. (Don't ask me where the pearls were!)

I was about to introduce myself to Saint Peter when I caught sight of a young girl: a corpse-like, emaciated creature with dark hair and haunted eyes. I gasped in horror, "Who are you?"

"I'm your facelift," she said. "I look like this because you had to look like that."

That girl was so real. She's somewhere, praying for her daily bread. I, who am wonderfully made, can indulge my vanity and buy some plastic surgeon's new speedboat. Or I can give that money to an organization that will feed her—and become *truly beautiful* in the eyes of God. I want to meet her at heaven's gate someday—to see how she looks after receiving my facelift money.

That vision convinced me more than anything that it is time to leave adolescence behind. So I'm trying something new these days. When I look in the mirror, I'm trying to see myself as God sees me. What are my best features? Do I have laughing eyes? A sweet smile? An air of wisdom about me? Do I project kindness? After I walk away from the mirror, I list all my activities, hobbies and friends. I think about projects I've completed, and the ones I look forward to. I think of good deeds I've been able to do, then dream up some new ones. Then I file this all away in that computer in my head under THINGS FOR WHICH TO BE THANKFUL.

When my birthday rolls around, I call up that file. Let friends and acquaintances send me silly cards with flaming birthday cakes and references to fire extinguishers. Let society tell me I'm losing value because I'm aging. My Creator and I both know better. I may be walking around in skin that looks like old underwear, but God doesn't care about my skin. He only cares about my heart. And if my Creator is not worrying about my skin, why should I?

Chapter 2

When Hot Nights Have Nothing to Do with Romance

"I CAN'T BE PREGNANT, I can't be pregnant. I cannot be pregnant." I repeated it like a litany. But this time common sense was no antidote for panic, and the words didn't make me feel any better. It was the spring of my thirty-eighth year and, although plenty of women my age were having babies, I did not want to be one of them. My bank account agreed.

How could this happen? I'd had my tubes tied, for crying out loud! (Which, incidentally, was what I was doing.) But things could come undone. My neighbor said her son's wife had her tubes tied, and she got pregnant. And if *she* could get pregnant. . . .

"You can't be pregnant," said my husband, trying to comfort me as I drove him to work. Just then the Baby Diaper Service truck rolled by, and I burst into fresh tears.

"Do you want me to stay home with you?" he asked, trying to be sensitive.

"No! Go away," said his appreciative wife.

He returned that night with a home pregnancy test.

I hadn't taken a test since college, but I passed this one with flying colors. I wasn't pregnant.

Odd. If I wasn't pregnant, what was I?

It took a few more months to figure it out: I was entering menopause, as in change of life, old broad, no more babies. (I didn't want any more, but knowing I couldn't if I *did* want a baby made me feel deprived.)

Experts say the first stage of loss is denial. I walked onto that stage, saying, "This can't be happening to me. I'm not even in my forties. I'm too young to go through menopause."

Not according to my mother. It appears that the women in our family like to wrap things up quickly. So here I was, starting to wrap things up.

Of course, I didn't figure this out immediately. I thought that a missed period was stress related. My life was so busy that I hardly had time to breathe—let alone track my menstrual cycle. As the year wore on, however, it began to dawn on me that I wasn't going through tampons as fast as I once did.

Still, I couldn't be entering menopause. Where were all the symptoms: the mood swings, the hot flashes where I'd turn beet red the supermarket line and sweat in front of strangers? Where was the depression? Where were the aches, pains and miseries I'd heard about? I wasn't having them, so I *couldn't* be menopausal.

Technically, I wasn't. I was *perimenopausal* (a fancy word for crossing the threshold), beginning to menstruate on a hit-and-miss basis. When it missed, it wasn't missed in the least. In fact, most of the participants in my survey agreed that no more periods was one of the bonuses of these middle years.

I do remember spending one whole summer waking up and kicking off blankets. I didn't associate that with menopause, even when I was still kicking off covers come fall—unusual behavior for a woman who had complained for years that she was freezing every time the thermostat dipped below sixty-five.

When a friend described her menopause experience to me, I realized she was describing me. *So it's happening*, I thought. The change of life. I'm officially aging. I'm no longer a sex symbol. I'll enter a room, and heads will no longer turn. (They never did anyway, but I'd always liked to pretend.)

My husband begged to differ with that conclusion; a middle-aged woman shedding not only the covers but her nightgown as well is still pretty sexy—at least to her middle-aged husband. Until she says, "Don't touch me! I'm so hot!" Too hot to handle—this is not how it reads in romance novels.

I realized that my biological reprogramming was affecting a lot more than my menstrual cycle. My libido was lower than a creek bed in August. Encounters of the close kind with my husband had been my favorite hobby in my twenties. Now, bed was the last place I wanted to spend time with him. I had other things to do.

As I mentioned in chapter one, I think this is God's way of directing us toward new vistas. It's not a shame to be less preoccupied with sex than when we were twenty. We now lack the biological need for coupling, so the hormones settle down and take a breather. (Since this is my theory, I won't be insulted if you think I'm nuts. Well, I might be insulted if you think I'm nuts. But I'll understand if you don't agree.) Irritating problems like vaginal dryness can make sexual encounters less pleasurable than those of earlier years too. This can make us less excited about intimacy.

If you are perimenopausal or menopausal, you may experience a general loss of energy and libido. These conditions may be treated. Have your hormone levels checked, and you might want to start with testosterone. Yes, *testosterone*. Women produce testosterone at a lower level than men, but we do produce some—and what we produce is very necessary. The production of testosterone in the adrenal glands begins puberty in boys and girls. Our ovaries primarily produce testosterone, from which estrogen is made.

Testosterone is a vital androgen (hormone) for men *and* for women. Some doctors burst out laughing at the suggestion of giving testosterone to women. So you might want to consider another hormone to increase libido: progesterone. This is a female hormone, and I guarantee it will be easier to get your doctor to prescribe it than testosterone.

Sometimes we suffer from more than a confused libido while our hormones sort things out. You may have noticed yourself becoming increasingly forgetful. I'll reach for a word I've been using since I was ten and come up empty-handed. Sometimes I leave my office on a mission to another part of the house, then forget what I was after. The I-have-too-much-on-my-mind excuse only covers so many of these aborted missions. I tried attributing my forgetfulness to genius. (They say Einstein was forgetful.) But I suspect it has more to do with low estrogen levels than a bulging brain.

These days you may often find yourself—what's that word for unhappy—oh, yes, depressed. One of my survey participants confesses, "At home, I just lost it. Everything I ever had pent up inside poured out in great waves," she says. "My family was shocked, and so was I." If you suffer similar troubles, or if you have night sweats, genital dryness or insomnia (I remember that one well!), you might want to look into taking supplemental estrogen.

The term "estrogen" refers to three major types of estrogen: estrone, estradiol and estriol. To simplify things, I'll refer to this team as estrogen. Not only does estrogen keep our reproductive cycle cycling, it is generally believed to be our best defense against osteoporosis. I say generally, because some physicians don't push for estrogen replacement. They figure that if you're exercising and getting plenty of calcium in your diet you'll be just fine.

Still, the specter of osteoporosis is scary. According to the National Osteoporosis Foundation, a woman's odds of fracturing her hip are equal to the combined risk of developing breast, uterine and ovarian cancer. Those of us at highest risk for bone fracture are white, petite women with small bones who hate exercise and have a low calcium intake. If we hit menopause before forty-five, we're in even bigger trouble.[1] On the bright side, the medical community has new drugs available to fight osteoporosis. Your doctor can give you the details.

For best results, estrogen replacement therapy should begin within three years of menopause. And you only receive the benefits as long as you take the hormone,[2] so once you get on that merry-go-round, ladies, you're there to stay.

Another consideration regarding estrogen replacement therapy is whether to use hormone replacement therapy (HRT, for short) or its alternative, natural replacement therapy (NRT). When you complain to your doctor about menopause miseries, chances are he will prescribe "traditional" (as in what the medical community has used since the 1940s) hormone therapy (HRT) for you. These synthetic hormones are manufactured by pharmaceutical companies from such interesting bases as the urine of pregnant mares. (Hence the name of one popular product, Premarin: Pre for pregnant, Mar for mares and In from Urine.)[3]

One thing to consider if you choose traditional hormone replacement therapy is the cancer question. In my research I found material as adamant *against* traditional HRT as I found *in favor* of it. One writer believes that pharmaceutical companies market HRT expressly to make a profit. The book cited several studies that pointed to estrogen as a possible cause of endometrial cancer. One study showed that women who had used synthetic estrogens for seven years or longer were fourteen times more likely to develop cancer of the uterine lining, or endometrium.[4] HRT enthusiasts claim that adding synthetic progesterone to the mix counteracts this problem.

The jury still seems to be out on whether traditional estrogen replacement causes breast cancer. Some sources admit it can but insist heart attacks pose a more serious threat. Also, cancer of the uterine lining can develop even in women who have never taken hormone supplements.[5] In fact, women who do *not* take HRT have a *greater* incidence of endometrial cancer than women who take estrogen and progesterone.[6]

However, if your family has a history of breast cancer, you might want to do some serious praying and thinking about this; other sources have pointed to an increased risk of about forty percent. That means when one woman in every 420 gets breast cancer at age sixty, one in every 300 women taking estrogen will develop it.[7]

My research revealed confusing and conflicting information on the side effects of HRT. That's why I decided to pass on it, put my aging body in God's hands and let nature take its course.

Speaking of nature—if your passage through menopause is rough, and you still want help, you can try natural hormone replacement (NRT). Natural hormones do not, as their patented sisters, have their origins in the urine of pregnant mares. Their source is a wild yam found in Mexico.

These tubers take a trip to a compounding lab, where scientists convert the phytoestrogen (plant estrogen) into human estrogen. The molecular structure of plant estrogen is the same as human estrogen, which is not at all the case with the animal-based hormones.[8]

Companies sometimes use the word "natural" loosely for promotion, as in the case of "wild Mexican yam cream" for sale in natural food or health stores. Sometimes these products contain synthesized progesterone added to the yam root extracts—without reporting the added hormone on the label.[9] The problem comes when Suzie Q. Customer smears on the cream. She thinks she is doing something good for her body. But unaware of what she's actually getting, she might mess up her hormonal balance. (As some ancient once said, let the buyer beware.)

Having sounded that note of caution, my research leads me to believe that fighting Mother Nature with natural hormones is better. They seem to cause less risk of cancer while providing the same amount of protection against osteoporosis. So, pass me a yam pill. And while you're at it, find something that takes away age spots and wrinkles. I guess even natural hormone replacement can't cure middle age.

And speaking of cures, contrary to what many medical journals might tell us, menopause is not a disease. It can't be, since no one has ever died from it.

In the first half of this century, menopause was considered a natural physiological event. Women were perfectly capable of coping without medical help. After scientists learned how to synthesize estrogen and progesterone, twentieth-century medicine decided menopause could be treated. If it was something that could be "treated," it must be a disease. Soon gynecologists were automatically prescribing estrogen for women.[10]

Well, you may be thinking, *it's easy for you to tell us that what we are experiencing is perfectly natural. But you're not lying in bed staring at the ceiling until 2:00 a.m., praying for sleep, or sledding ice cubes up and down your neck to cool down a hot flash.*

I'm not saying, "It's natural—so suffer." There are many natural remedies to alleviate menopausal symptoms. Vitamins E and B6, for instance, as well as herbs.

If you'd like to experiment with herbs, here are a few I learned about:

- Panax Ginseng is said to help relieve vaginal dryness and pain during intercourse.
- Black Cohosh (*Cimicifuga racemosa*) is a Native American discovery for relief of menstrual cramps and is considered useful against menopause-related depression.
- *Dong Quai* and Licorice stimulate estrogen action. (In other words, they get moving what feeble amounts you have left!)

If osteoporosis concerns you, changes in diet may do wonders for your bones—and take you out of the cancer roulette that appears to come with synthetic hormones. Before trying any herb, however, be sure to check with your physician.

Add Phytoestrogens

A group of investigators discovered that Japanese women don't suffer from hot flashes the way their American sisters do. They found that Japanese women have a very high intake of phytoestrogens (100 to 1,000-fold more than American women).[11] Increasing our intake of phytoestrogens will compensate for our body's slowdown in production of estrogen. Phytoestrogens are associated with soy products, such as tofu, miso, aburage, koridofu, soybeans and sprouted soybeans. Two ounces daily of tofu or other exotic soy goodies may ward off hot flashes and other menopause miseries and perhaps even protect against cancer and heart disease.[12]

One friend shared her recipe for a phytoestrogen pick-me-up: one-half cup soy milk, one-half to one cup milk (and don't use nonfat milk; your body needs those fats to help it absorb calcium!), one banana and one package of breakfast drink mix. Whip this in the blender, then drink. My son and I tried this by substituting two-and-a-half tablespoons of soy powder for the soy milk and increasing the milk. Not bad. Other phytoestrogens are black cohosh and licorice (mentioned above), alfalfa sprouts and pomegranates (which, incidentally, were a symbol of fertility in ancient times).

Take Your Vitamins

Vitamin D is the main regulator of calcium. Get out in the sun for half an hour and you'll get 300 to 350 units of it. Cod liver oil is also a good source of Vitamin D. (That stuff tastes nasty, but you can get it in capsules.) Vitamin A enables your intestinal walls to absorb nutrients, and you can find it in yellow and deep green vegetables and in fruit. Vitamin E enables you to utilize the estrogen stores in your adrenal or fat tissues. It also slows the process of skin wrinkling! A deficiency in this vitamin is associated with breast cancer.[13]

Take Your Minerals

Potassium, magnesium and little known minerals like silicon and boron are all essential to good health. Did you know, for instance, that magnesium plays an important role in converting vitamin D to its active form?[14]

Say "No" to Bone-Breakers

Soda pop, sugar and caffeine are all detrimental to your bones. Sugar increases calcium excretion. Soda is high in phosphorous, and too much soda pop prevents the proper assimilation of new calcium into our bones. Coffee and caffeine subtly damage bones too.[15] Cut down on your meat intake. Too much protein causes calcium to be lost in the urine. As a general rule, no more than one and one-half ounces of protein are required for a 150 pound person per day.[16]

Get Moving

In addition to diet, other recommendations can also help. They are continued sexual activity (my husband was glad to hear that), endorphin-producing pursuits and regular exercise. Even if you are not a candidate for the United States Olympic Team, you can still exercise. Walking three hours a week cuts the risk of heart attack and stroke forty percent in women ages forty to sixty-five. Also, women who walk forty to forty-five minutes five times a week are sick with colds or flu half as often as sedentary women. You can lose about eighteen pounds a year without dieting if you walk forty-five minutes four times a week.[17]

Are you saying, "Never mind the diet and exercise. How do I get hold of this natural hormone stuff?" Contact the American College for Advancement in Medicine. This organization will help you find a doctor who will test your hormone levels and, if necessary, prescribe natural hormone therapy. The address and telephone are:

American College for Advancement
in Medicine
23121 Verdugo Dr. Suite 204
Laguna Hills, CA 92653
Internet: www.acam.org
Phone: 1-800-532-3688

And no, they are not giving me a kickback for the promo. The views expressed in this book on natural hormone replacement therapy do not reflect the views of this station or my publisher. That should take care of the disclaimers. I just thought some of my readers might find this information helpful.

Here's another bit of information you might find helpful as well. *Nutraceuticals* (the latest arrival on the preventive medicine scene) are food supplements with proven health effects. They support the endocrine system's natural production and balance of hormones. They also help the body with physical and emotional stress. Stabilized *dioscorea* complex (remember our wild Mexican yam?) along with *Ambrotose,* a recent *gylconutritional* discovery, provide natural raw materials for our bodies to make needed hormones and deliver them where required. *Ambrotose*, I have learned, also provides the monosaccharides (how's that for a mouthful!) our bodies need for cell to cell communication. Good communication between our cells means a healthy immune system.

The scientist who invented *Ambrotose* joined doctors and executives to form a company (it's the American way, after all!) to sell this product. I have been using the stuff and have found that it has increased my energy level. I still don't look like I'm twenty, but I feel like it. (If you would like to explore this option, you can get more information by contacting Randal or Marcia Jones at 1-888-844-6556.)

I'd like to add a postscript about hormonally-based depression. If you eat well and have mastered the hormonal balancing act—remember, depression can be related to the circumstances of our age as well as our hormones or lack of them. Some of these may be the empty nest, aging parents, a husband's midlife crisis, or dissatisfaction with work.[18]

The more I researched all possible dangers of HRT and the things I'd have to give up to balance my hormones naturally, the more depressed I became.

Until I remembered two inescapable facts. After Eve blew it in the garden, we humans became much like our appliances—built to break down. "Dust you are and to dust you will return," God said to Adam (Genesis 3:19). We are all slowly dying, and no amount of hormones, wonder drugs or trips to the gym will change that fact. All things die. But even as we wind down toward death, we approach new, indestructible, eternal life. Paul says, in First Corinthians 15:53-54: "For the perishable must clothe itself with the imperishable, and the mortal with immortality. When the perishable has been clothed with the imperishable, and the mortal with immortality, then the saying that is written will come true: 'Death has been swallowed up in victory.' " There will be no such thing as death in heaven, or age spots or wrinkles or widow's humps or broken bones.

And that brings me to my second comforting fact: God, my Heavenly Father, holds my tomorrows, and that includes both my middle and my aged years. For all I know, I may not have any aged years. I could die in a plane crash next month, fall off a mountain or be hit by a car while walking down the road. But whatever happens to this mortal body, this time-scored casing, the real me, my soul, will remain intact because my soul belongs to God. "Neither death nor life, neither angels nor demons, neither the present nor the future, nor any powers, neither height nor depth, nor anything else in all creation, will be able to separate us from the love of God that is in Christ Jesus our Lord" (Romans 8:38).

I'm happy to announce that all those irritating menopause symptoms have subsided. I am no longer lying awake at night wondering if I drank too much caffeine, and I am not kicking off the covers anymore. I'm still rarely cold (which is a real treat, and probably my body's last hurrah before old age and poor circulation render me constantly cold).

I have come to look at menopause as a river we must cross to a new land. For some of us, that crossing can be miserable. If you are in misery, take a hormonal or homeopathic seasick pill with my blessing, and know that you will survive the journey. We all do. Take it from those of us who have made it to the other side. Life is just as exciting on this bank!

Chapter 3

Mother, May I?

 "IT'S NINE O'CLOCK, TIME for bed," I said. "Go brush your teeth, and put on your jammies."

"But I'm twenty," protested my daughter.

"Oh. Yeah." I brushed my teeth, put on my jammies and went to bed, leaving my daughter to turn out the lights and lock up.

It's strange to reach the point where your children want to be treated like adults. After years of being the commander general, I'm suddenly supposed to stop? I am an expert on what is best for them. I've got to admit that there have been times recently when I've become frustrated because the little ingrates showed a distinct disinclination to follow my advice.

Actually the teen years wouldn't be so bad—if our offsprings' maturity matched their independent attitude. But they don't, even at eighteen—the magic age when the legal fairy waves her magic wand and says, "You're an adult. Poof!" I'd love to meet the lawmakers who plucked "eighteen" out of the air and said, "This works." They had not met my daughter, Honey, and her friends.

Honey has, for the most part, kept her nose clean (both figuratively and literally). In this day of drug and alcohol abuse, that's an accomplishment. But she's managed to find her share of mischief. She is taking increasingly more responsibility for her own life, but she still doesn't think like a middle-aged woman.

Because my children and I look at life from different perspectives, I have "A" rules and "B" rules. My children know that these rules exist for two reasons. First, they live in my house: it's my game board, and I get to make the rules. Second, as a middle-aged woman, I need things to run smoothly and calmly. That is how I stay sane.

The "A" rules smack of "A" type personalities. These cover such areas as neatness. Chores must be done and rooms kept up. The rule regarding rooms has always caused the most friction. In fact, you would think after all this time I'd have given up. But hey, I'm no quitter. "It's my room," protests my daughter when the neatness patrol sweeps through.

"Which is in my house," I reply.

I did try the old "shut the door" routine that so many experts advise. But the smell continued to creep from under their doors, like smoke. Allowing my offspring to wallow in a filthy cage wasn't creating good hygiene habits. I expected them to brush their teeth and take baths regularly, so would it make sense to allow them to recreate the Love Canal in their bedrooms?

I decided to tackle this problem once and for all—especially with my oldest who would not be at home to nag—I mean, help—much longer. I hit her where it hurt—her pocketbook. "Every time I find your room a mess, I'm going to fine you five bucks," I announced. "I will burn any clothes I pick off the floor. If you find yourself buck naked, you'll have to finance a new wardrobe."

This has somewhat worked. I no longer find clothes scattered about the floor; now they spill from her drawers. She's been a sport about the fines. The one time I enforced it, we blew my windfall on ice cream. (Sometimes these things work better in theory than in practice.)

We are seeing improvement. My daughter is finally getting organized. She has invested in plastic storage containers to pack up everything from stuffed animals to old shoes. Although our definitions of clean may never be the same, when she finally has her own place, I don't have to visit. We can meet somewhere for lunch. That way I won't risk tripping over a soda pop can and breaking my neck.

Another of my "A" rules insists that my little dears not play their music at an ear-splitting level and further deafen their parents, who are both experiencing hearing problems (which probably started when those parents were teenagers and listening to music at ear-splitting levels).

Type "B" rules are the biggies. They center on things like keeping curfews and informing parents of their whereabouts. I don't think my little dears would stay out until all hours playing mailbox baseball, but you never know. (For the uninitiated, mailbox baseball involves as many teenagers as can fit into a car. They cruise rural roads taking wild swings with a baseball bat at mailboxes. Every time I drive past a dented mailbox, I long to see the mailbox owners allowed into the perpetrators' homes to play boom box baseball. They don't call me Old Bat for nothing!)

Teens and parents look at time so differently. Teens who are having a wonderful time with friends know they are safe. Parents, however—lonely and with no life of their own—start to grow restless around 11:30. Overactive imaginations run rampant (What else have they but imagination? Certainly no money with which to go out and have their own fun—they gave it all to the kids). They wonder if the car is acting up. Nasty little phrases like "date rape" haunt their minds. By midnight these poor parents are calculating: the movie finished at 11:00, they stopped for a hamburger for half an hour, thirty minutes to drive home. . . . Now the parents start to pace. Their hearts don't settle back to a normal pace until that car finally pulls up.

Which is why we need curfews. That way we know when to start worrying and pacing, and maybe we can at least enjoy part of our "old person" rented video and fat-free microwave popcorn.

One friend suggested an idea. Mom and Dad (also known as Old Bat and Mr. Lemon) set their bedside alarm for 11:00 p.m., midnight, 1:00 p.m.—whatever hour Cinderella turns into a pumpkin. They then cuddle up and go blissfully to sleep. It is Cinderella's job to get home and turn off the alarm before it wakens the sleeping monsters. If the alarm goes off, Mr. Lemon and Old Bat immediately call every person Cinderella has ever known—followed by the police and the National Guard—thus making a great stir and embarrassing Cinderella in front of all her peers.

This works wonderfully with teens. With older children you may as well just give them a house key and ask them to be quiet coming home. Hopefully, older children have already moved out because your rules have driven them nuts, and they had to get away. (Another benefit of rules.)

Speaking of rules, I have noticed that there is still often confusion over them—even though I have been perfectly clear. My words get twisted and I, somehow, get blamed for wrong or lacking decisions. Rather than squabble, I finally wrote out a few rules and regulations, "For Of-Age Individuals living at the old Rabe Boarding House." These included a page of rules regarding work, attitudes and household responsibilities. Now, everybody's clear on what is required. It eliminates excuses.

Sometimes rules alone aren't the source of friction between parent and growing child. Hormones (ours and theirs) can help create fireworks. That, combined with our children's feeling that we just aren't listening, may reduce their affection toward us. When a child says, "I'm stupid," she may be really saying, "Help me succeed." That plea might mean getting a tutor, pulling her out of a class or trying an alternative method of schooling.

As for those teenage tirades, we'll live a lot longer if we can learn to take them with a grain of salt. This has always been hard for me to do. Like Aretha Franklin, I'm a big believer in "R-E-S-P-E-C-T." And my feelings are easily hurt. So it took me years to learn that emotions and hormones can lead teenagers to say inane things they don't really mean.

I've found it helpful to step back and ask, "Is this behavior rebellious, spiritually threatening or just plain stupid?" When my son came home from his best friend's house with neon-yellow hair, I was not thrilled. But this behavior came under the category of stupid, so I learned to live with it. (We also had the beautician help him look less like a walking light bulb.) And, looking on the bright side, we are reducing the electric bill. When we want to read at night, we simply ask Junior to come in and stand around.

With all we parents endure when they live at home, you wouldn't think it possible that we could suffer when our offspring finally depart. But we do, and psychologists have labeled it *empty-nest syndrome*. One mother once wrote me, "I don't feel needed anymore . . . no more babies to cuddle, no more little hands to hold. I ask myself what my future will be. What am I good for?"

Good question. For those of us who feel that motherhood was our life's calling, what do we do when there is no one left to mother? The realization that we are no longer the center of our children's universe can be painful.

When my son talks enthusiastically about the day he moves out, I feel hurt. *He loves me so little that he can hardly wait to leave*, I think in a maudlin moment. But that is not the case. My son is only doing what he is supposed to do: preparing to take responsibility for his own life. The fact that he is excited to begin his great adventure says he is confident and ready to strike out on his own. When my job to raise and nurture him is done, he must leave me and live the life to which God has called him.

We'll talk more later about life after children. For now, if you are a nurturer suddenly out of a job, I can guarantee God will bring more people into your life who need nurturing. Our heavenly Father is always pleased when we say to him, "I've finished the task you set before me. I'm ready for a new assignment."

Others suffer from an entirely different midlife malady. Joyce answered my survey question, "What particularly bothers you about your age?" this way: "Gray hair, wrinkles and a fear that my children are going to live at home forever." Doctor Sheila (that's me) has labeled this attitude *full-nest syndrome*, and I'm suffering from it even as I write this book.

Full-nest syndrome produces feelings of frustration and depression in parents whose children *haven't* moved out and show no intention of doing so. In nests all across America, big birdlings have decided it is better to stay with Mommy and Daddy Bird than to fly out and get eaten by a cat. Besides, it's so much trouble to collect all those twigs and feathers and build a nest. In fact, it's work. Why work when the nest you're in does just fine?

If this scenario sounds familiar, let me say that in most cases adult children do eventually strike out on their own. If your child shows no desire to fly into the cold, cruel world, he probably doubts that his wings will hold him airborne. Some kids know from the age of ten what they want to do with their lives. The array of options stuns others. Maybe your child is one of those. As has been the case with our daughter, you may need to help your Junior outline a plan of action. Suggest he devote two days a week to investigating careers, sending for college and vocational school catalogs or visiting schools.

Maybe one of his hobbies might lead to a paying job. A kid who enjoys animals, for instance, might want to work or volunteer in a veterinary hospital. Junior can also set up an appointment with a counselor at the local community college. At a vocational school, our daughter, Honey, took a C.O.P.S. test to help find jobs that line up with her interests.

If you suspect that all this prevaricating has more to do with laziness than with confusion and fear, help your child set goals and deadlines. "If you are going to school by fall, we won't charge you rent." "If you don't have a job by summer, you will work for Dad—chopping wood, painting the house, weeding the flowers and mowing the lawn for $10.00 a week. Hope you'll be able to pay for your car insurance!" This veiled threat will hopefully remind your big bird that growing up requires adult responsibilities as well as adult privileges.

If you perceive that your bird is ready to fly, you may have to push her out of the nest so she can exercise those wings. Charging rent is a good beginning. If this seems callous, you can put that money into a savings account. Then, present it to your offspring on moving day—which will come much sooner than if she's allowed to stay for free indefinitely. Again, remember the joy of rules. If Junior complains about his curfew, point out that when he's on his own he won't have one. Sooner or later, the call of independence will lure him toward self-sufficiency.

Those of us suffering from full-nest syndrome need to examine the causes. It's one thing to help our children stand on their own. It's quite another to want them out because we don't want to look like parental failures. It took me awhile to figure that out. After Honey graduated from high school, friends and relatives asked, "What now?" We couldn't provide that information because Honey had no idea. "Well, she can't just do nothing," was the general consensus.

They're right, I thought. *She can't do* nothing. "Honey, what are you going to do?" I'd demand.

"I don't know," Honey would reply.

At which point I would share my philosophy of life at a decibel she was sure to hear, "Well, do something, even if it's wrong!" (The underlying message: Get your act together, and quit embarrassing me in front of my friends.)

So Honey started working part-time and studying a book on finding a career focus, *What Color is Your Parachute?* Now she has two part-time jobs and is taking classes at the community college but still hasn't found her career direction. When we ask if she's figured out the color of her parachute, she replies that it's black. Well, black, pink, orange, I don't care—just so it eventually opens.

Meanwhile, her room in the family plane is here—as long as she fulfills her obligations as part of the household. You hear that, Honey? And that cool book I found for you at the library, *Escape to Freedom*, was not a hint to move out. Really!

I've come to the conclusion that friends and relatives—no matter how well meaning—may not know our children as well as we do. Although we can thank them for their input, we don't necessarily need to let that input drive us to start packing Junior's suitcase. If a child has suffered failures in school or lost a job, he may not have the confidence to strike out on his own. Or if your child bit off more academically than he could chew and burned out, he may need a few months to recharge his batteries before getting back on the academic treadmill. Your relatives can't know what is going on in your child's head. You might not even know. So pray before following any well-meant advice.

We also can't shove our children out of the house simply because they are beginning to get on our nerves or because we are longing for room to stretch, even though these developments often make the parting less painful. If irritation were a legitimate reason, both my children would be out the door. My grocery budget, like the national debt, shows no sign of getting under control.

And Honey's pet rats—there's a subject that raises my blood pressure. Honey's father gave her Rat A, also known as Basil, so he was highly cherished. He was very cute (for a rat) and so that worked against me also. My daughter purchased Rat B, Chewy, because Basil was lonely. We couldn't have Basil lonely, now could we? Never mind the fact that Mom is going nuts! Well, Basil has gone on to his great reward. We buried him next to the cat: enemies in life, friends in death. But there's still Chewy: hale, hearty and smelly.

Every time I walk past my daughter's room, I smell eau de rat. I have to fight the temptation to slip rodent killer into the little boy's food dish. I tell myself that soon Honey will be out on her own, and rat boy will move with her. She will come home to visit and leave the grandrat behind. But since Honey is still not sure what she wants to do when she grows up, who knows how long it will be before she finds her own nest. Meanwhile, the walls (and the rat) keep closing in on me.

Living with teenagers can be difficult. Because of their grown-up bodies and occasionally grown-up behavior, we begin to think they're just like us. But they won't act like us for at least twenty years. It's easy to forget what we were like at sixteen or eighteen or twenty. We say, "Junior will not drive like a maniac, cut class or skateboard behind a moving car." (Of course he will, because he is acting just like we did thirty-some years ago.) Our own confused expectations make parenting difficult at this time of life. When we have more reasonable (translation: tolerant) expectations for our young, everyone is happier.

Most of the time, Honey and I converse like two reasonable adults. When we're in the middle of a positive time, I say to myself, *This is so good.* Other times we get into arguments over everything from what she wears to what she eats. *Do I really want to engage in these stupid arguments?* I ask myself.

I don't. So, I'm trying to keep my mouth shut more. (Honey would disagree, I'm sure. If she only knew how many times I want to say something and don't!) And when my daughter comes to me for advice, I try to give her just that—and not a lecture. Advice says, "If I were you . . ." or "You might try . . ." or "I don't think I'd . . . and here's why." It doesn't say, "Don't," "You shouldn't" or "You need to."

In my survey, I noticed that there seemed to be a consensus on this strategy. One mother observed, "The younger teens still need more 'molding,' usually by discussing a situation or behavior. The older ones (by eighteen or nineteen years) really resent too much of Mom and Dad's opinion about anything, which is probably a normal part of pulling away and tackling life with their own hands and brains." She continued, "I have seen parents persist [until] the child is almost forced to continue in [their] direction . . . just to prove their parents wrong."

In her survey response, Becky Gorton points out that she and her husband offer more opinions and advice to their nineteen-year-old than to their older children. She explains, "We maintain that right because we're still financially supporting her."

Good point. I often hear radio talk show psychologists tell complaining parents that their teenager (even those still living at home) is his or her own person. Frankly, if one of my offspring used that argument on me, it would convulse me with laughter. That's a little hard to take seriously when he's living under my roof, eating my food and putting his dirty clothes in my hamper. Still, treating our children with respect, politely asking them to do things, and thanking them for a job well-done is not hard to do. And it gets better results.

As long as my children are under my roof, I figure I should be allowed to polish the little gems. However, nagging them doesn't foster a burning desire to improve, either. So, I've tried to disguise my polishing efforts. "Hey, I'm almost done in the bathroom, then it's all yours so you can GET A BATH." (I'm happy to announce that, as of this writing, my little gems are both clean and shiny.)

Bribery, for some reason, is never considered an insult. For example: "Look, it really bugs me when you slouch, so let's make a deal. For every day you keep your back straight, I'll give you a dollar." I seem to be constantly broke, so I've found the money method difficult. But I could possibly bribe my kids with non-monetary treats. "For every day you don't slouch, I'll do one of your chores for you." "If you keep your room neat for one week, I'll bake you chocolate chip cookies."

On the opposite end of motivation stands negative reinforcement. One of my survey respondents suggested threatening removal of financial support to get a teen to tow the line. "If you want us to keep paying for your college education . . ."

Guilt also motivates, but it's one I'd use sparingly. We run to pleasure and away from pain, and it is easy to tell into which category a guilt-inflicting mother falls. I want to change my children's behavior not douse their enjoyment of my company!

With older teens, the best teacher is often experience (just like it is for us). If either of my children gets a speeding ticket, guess who pays for it? The same goes for any damages done to the car when a teen was at the wheel. Honey and Junior now each have their own cars, for which they pay the insurance, license tags and repair bills.

Learning by experience can also apply to larger financial issues. Bruce Williams, popular radio personality and financial expert, cautions parents against co-signing on their children's loans. . . unless, of course, you would like to own a fire-red pickup truck or another house. (Hey, you can always rent out the house!)

Learning from mistakes is painful, but nothing teaches the meaning of "hot" like burning your hand. More than a thousand lectures, getting burned financially will teach our children how to be cautious with money. The same holds true for their friendships, romantic relationships and career choices.

Our children will ultimately decide where to attend church. After Honey graduated from high school, she was the only college-aged person left at our church. "There's no one my age here," she complained. "I want to go to the church down the road where my friends are going."

"Oh, no you don't," was our instant reply. Our church had suffered an ugly split two years earlier, and to allow our daughter to attend somewhere else seemed, somehow, disloyal. Besides, we were a family. Families go to the same church. Together. Right?

Yes, probably, in a perfect world. But this is not a perfect world, and we decided that it was better to see our daughter enthusiastic about church instead of being a body in a pew with her mind a million miles away. Shortly after this, I read an article that confirmed that, in our case, we had made a good decision. The writer said, "Making a conscious choice of where and how to worship God is a step each maturing Christian must take."[1] A time will come when our children must stake their own claim to faith. In our case, this has been positive. Our daughter has found a great new group of friends and new excitement about her faith.

Watching a child learn to walk the slender thread of life can be nerve-racking. Every time that child loses his balance, you think he's going to break his neck for sure. It seems that every household has at least one child who is the designated gray-hair giver, the one you worry about and pray about the most. Motherly instinct says, "Catch that child—he's going to fall!" Taking the final step into adulthood is like working a high-wire act; in the end, we all have to learn to balance.

As they learn to balance, we have to allow our kids to make missteps. A good example is the story of the prodigal son. He squandered his inheritance on good times and then found himself sleeping with the pigs (See Luke 15:11-32). Our children often have to see the dividends of poor choices before they admit their error and change.

Hitting bottom these days can be a lot uglier than anything the prodigal ever faced. In those days, a man might drink too much wine and fall off his donkey on a lonely road. Today, our prodigal son consumes a quantity of alcohol much higher than his biblical counterpart, then climbs into a metal killing-machine that can go eighty to a hundred miles an hour. If he doesn't fall prey to alcohol, drugs will leave him in a continual stupor—or even claim his life. I'm no psychologist, but I believe if a child is drifting into life-threatening behavior, then a parent needs to intervene.

If I were a parent to a prodigal in danger, before running to my local shrink, I'd run to God. He knows the human mind better than any other and knows best what a parent should do. James 1:5 promises that if we lack wisdom, we can come to our heavenly Father, and he will give it to us. The best course to take whenever we're worried about our children is to pray first. (With all the wisdom requests I've put in over the years, I should be second only to Solomon!) My survey participants agreed that prayer best hauls our children back from the edge of the cliff.

When our children finally get smart (translation: come around to our way of thinking) we need the grace not to say, "I told you so." Whenever I talk about graciousness toward our offspring, I think of my friend Marge. She was determined to teach her engaged daughter how to cook. Marge's in-laws were caterers, and Marge has set the table for many important affairs. She always brings several amazing dishes to a potluck. "She's going to learn to make pie before she's married," vowed Marge. But Pie Making 101 was canceled due to lack of interest.

Lo and behold, only a month after the wedding, her daughter called Marge in a panic. "We're having a big dinner, and I'm supposed to bring the pie. Mom, can you show me how?"

Can you imagine the temptation to say, "Didn't I tell you . . . ?" Instead, Marge said, "I'll be right over." She and her newly married daughter had a great time at Pie Making 101.

We must be ever vigilant regarding our children's spiritual life. Eli, the priest, is a sad biblical example of a wimpy parent. Eli's wicked sons didn't take their offices as spiritual leaders seriously,[2] and instead of removing them, Eli let them remain. They committed sexual sin and robbed the people they were supposed to serve. God called Eli on his inaction. In First Samuel 2:29, He demands, "Why do you honor your sons more than me . . . ?"

Why, indeed? Do we as parents ever wimp out? Have you avoided talking with your older teen or adult child about sexual sin or drifting away from church? It's easy to tell a six-year-old to go to the corner and think about his naughty behavior, but what about a twenty-five-year- old? That child can say, "If you feel that way, I just won't come over. And I won't bring your grandchildren, either." We hesitate to correct our grown children because we fear we'll lose them. But as Eli learned, it is better to alienate them in this life than lose them eternally.

I know I'm more open to gentle and insightful criticism, backed up with Scripture and reason. We are all sheep who often wander too close to the edge of the cliff. When helping our children, we can be firm but gentle—and not judgmental. If they remain stubborn in their sin, we can pray that God will bring them to their knees—and then brace for the crash.

Meanwhile, we don't have to support them in their wrongdoing. Our friend, Mike, informed his daughter and her fiancé that if they continued to live together he could not in good conscience walk his daughter down the aisle. The fiancé moved out immediately. I applaud Mike's stand for righteousness.

When we close our eyes to our children's wrong behavior, as Eli did, we make their love an idol and worship it with our inaction. God told Eli, regarding his offspring, "Every one of you that I do not cut off from my altar will be spared only to blind your eyes with tears and to grieve your heart" (1 Samuel 2:33).

Eli isn't the only example of bad parenting in the Bible. First Kings 1:6 tells us that King David avoided disciplining his son, Adonijah, probably for the same reason as parents today—he adored his son and wanted that feeling reciprocated. He'd already lost Absalom, who was killed as he revolted against David. Also, the Bible tells us that Adonijah was a golden boy. I can imagine the aging David looking at his handsome son and saying, "He's really a good boy." That may have been David's opinion, but the unbiased writer of First Kings didn't share it.

There may be times when, although we've tried to train our children according to Proverbs 22:6, they still rebel. A godly woman named Monica had a son who seemed determined to break her heart. He rejected her faith and followed in his unbelieving father's footsteps. Once—just for the joy of it—he stole some pears. When the son grew to manhood, he moved in with a girl—the first of many. He jokingly prayed, "Give me chastity—only not yet." But his mother never stopped praying, and at age thirty-three he gave his life to God. We have no way of knowing how many people he influenced for good through the years, but most of us know him: Saint Augustine.

You may be thinking, *I'd have more hope if I'd been a better parent.* Maybe you came to know our Lord, the Christ, when your children were nearly grown. Perhaps you didn't focus enough on helping your children form godly habits. No matter what our failures, God can redeem them. We can always hold up the tangled skein of our lives and plead, "Please, fix it." That might involve asking your children's forgiveness for your mistakes.

There is nothing so bad that God can't use it for good. I read about the Lundstroms, popular gospel singers and evangelists who, watched their daughter slip away. She ended up in prostitution. How could anything good come out of that! But after much prayer and pain, their daughter returned to her family and her faith. God now uses her to help others through a radio program she shares with her dad.

It is our responsibility to pray for our children, to counsel them and take a stand against immoral behavior. But responsibility for their choices, ultimately, is theirs. God tells us in Ezekiel 18:4, "The soul who sins is the one who will die." The chapter also talks about the good man who has a son who does wrong. "Will such a man live?" demands God, speaking of that violent son. "He will not! Because he has done all these detestable things, he will surely be put to death and *his blood will be on his own head*" (18:13, emphasis added). No one will stand before God's judgment seat and blame another for his own wrongdoing. Acknowledge your mistakes, yes. But don't take full responsibility for the choices your grown children make in life.

Something else which is likely to come up with grown children is the in-law issue. I want to be like my own mother-in-law, who has never given me unasked-for advice. Her underlying message has always been: I see this woman as my own daughter. Mom made sure I knew that right from the start. The Christmas that we announced our engagement, she hurried out and bought something to place under her Christmas tree for me.

Someone must have passed on to her the mother-in-law code of honor. The woman who lives by this code doesn't point out to her son his wife's faults. She doesn't expect her son to take her side against his wife or expect to come first in a married child's life. This mother-in-law sees the good in every addition to the family, even if she secretly wonders what her child ever saw in that turkey. She knows that in the drama that is her child's marriage, she is a supporting actress—not the star. We haven't all inherited this kind of mother-in-law, but we can live by her code.

If you are one of the many these days entering middle age with younger children, you won't have to deal with the issues of (nearly) adult children for some time. Instead you are finding that a young family at this stage of life comes with its own mixed blessings.

You may be more financially secure, yet you may wonder how you'll cope with teenagers when you are close to retirement. You may find that child rearing is especially exhausting now. If you find yourself running out of steam, I suggest you remember the magic words that never failed me (until recently): I'm tired. Go to bed.

This chapter has looked at some of the negatives of having grown or nearly grown children. But there are many positives as well.

When my offspring were little, we played Chutes and Ladders and had tea parties, complete with mud pies. My husband pretended to be the Big Wolf and chased the kids around. I can still remember their squeals. That was entertaining for the time. But as our children grew, we found more activities we could enjoy together. We introduced more complex games and the joys of travel to them. In turn, we acquired some of their interests. My daughter brought volleyball home to us. For the last two years, she and I have played on a team together. Not only do I enjoy spending time with her but I have learned a new skill. Shared talents create a bond too. Junior and I enjoy talking about songwriting and cool guitar riffs. Music is a joy we'll share for years to come.

I have invested many years in raising two wonderful children, and now I get to enjoy them on a whole new level, as *lifelong friends*. I pray the same for every other mother my age—if not now, then in the near future.

Chapter 4

Grandmothering:
The Great Frontier

May you live to see your children's children.

Psalm 128:6

THESE DAYS, I KISS my son on the cheek at the risk of getting whisker burn. He is big and manly—and not ashamed to hug his mother. But the only person he cuddles with now is his girlfriend. Even if he were willing, I wouldn't risk him sitting on my lap. He would squish me. My daughter has always been affectionate, but she has finally taken my advice to get a life. She is never home. So I have no one to nurture but the cat. (Well, the rat too, but I am not that desperate!)

This, I have concluded, is why we need grandchildren.

Grandmotherhood is the step after motherhood for many of us. And, like motherhood, it comes with its own set of job requirements. I am not yet there, so I asked several experts (real-life grandmothers) for their opinions on the fine art of grandmothering.

They agreed that being a grandmother gives double the pleasure. You can enjoy your offspring's children—and give them back before the thrill wears off. Here is how the grandmothers I talked to defined themselves:

Grandmothers are usually happy and cuddly.

A lot of kids like to hug their grandmas, and grandmas like to hug their grandchildren. A child happily anticipates going to Grandma's house. In a child's mind, "Grandma" equals warmth, security and deep contentment.

Grandmothers are not as strict as mothers.

The grandmas I talked to do not run houses with no rules, but they do have fewer rules.

One grandmother related that after a visit to her house, her grandson left his clothes in a heap on his bedroom floor. "Pick up your clothes," said Mom.

"I don't have to pick them up at Grandma's," replied her son.

I'll bet you can guess what his mother's reply was, and yes, he did pick up his clothes.

At Grandma's house you may not have to clean your room, or your plate, or worry about spoiling your appetite with a late afternoon candy bar.

Grandmothers listen.

They don't usurp a mother's position, but they want to listen to a grandchild's troubles and offer advice if asked. Many times Honey hiked up the road to Grandma's house to pour out her troubles when things weren't going well at school or she and Mom had fought.

Grandmothers keep confidences.

My mother, I'm sure, has heard some interesting tales. I know that if a child confided a drug or other serious problem to her, she would have no compunction about turning stool pigeon. But for the less serious secrets she proved herself a safe repository to two generations of grandchildren.

Grandmothers take time.

Everyone else is busy trying to earn a living, clean the house and get to softball practice, soccer practice or music lessons. Grandmothers may be the last line of defense against the child-gobbling whirlpool of busyness. Grandma takes time to sit with her grandchild in a big, stuffed armchair to read a story. Grandma shows you how to roll out a pie crust or takes you on a walk to collect autumn leaves.

Grandma isn't trying to make payments on a house and a minivan. She understands the value of slowing down and taking time to enjoy life. And if another human being understands enjoying life, it's a child. That makes grandchild and grandparent a perfect match!

Here are tips I gleaned on how to be a good grandmother. (If you are already doing them, congratulations! You earn a grandmothering gold medal.)

Leave the door open a crack.

Any bedroom can be a scary place at night when you're small. My son tells me now that he was terrified to sleep in my old bedroom at Grandma's house because of a stuffed owl she stored there. That thing came to life every time we went to visit Grandma, and he was never quite able to explain to Grandpa why he kept creeping down the stairs to the safety of the light and the grown-ups. Maybe that was because Grandpa kept chasing him back up the stairs, growling, "Get in bed!"

Always have popsicles.

Grandma's house has treats, great smells and fun times. For kids, great times don't have to cost a lot. A popsicle is hot stuff when you're five.

Smile at dirty clothes.

You can do that now, you know. You don't have to fuss and worry over Suzie's new outfit. You didn't buy it—and you've learned that Suzie is more important than the clothes she's wearing.

Relax and enjoy.

Now that you have time, you can do outings with the grandkids that you always wanted to do with the kids: lunch out at a fancy tea room, a trip to the art museum, hide-and-seek in the back yard.

When I see a harried mother snapping at her children, I want to put my arm around her and say, "Please don't. You'll look back someday, relive every harsh word you uttered and be so sorry. You are the sun these little ones revolve around, and your approval means so much. Those older women who said they grow up so fast were right. Love these little ones now while you have the chance."

So far, I haven't done this. I'm a gutless coward and don't want to get punched in the nose. But I am going to work up my nerve one of these days and do it.

Were you one of those harried, snappish moms? You don't have to hurry now, and you don't have to snap. You can meander down the river of life and allow your grandchildren to bob along in your gentle wake. In this crazy world, you may be their only peaceful harbor.

Spoil 'em and send 'em home.

Children need someone who will give them a second helping of pie or let them stay up past their bedtime. Do it. Walk on the edge. When the kids have worn you out, you can wave good-bye, kick off your shoes and collapse on the couch with a cup of tea.

Not every grandmother can send her grandkids home these days. In some cases, grandma's house *is* home. The sixties produced more than hippies and tie-dyed clothes. It produced irresponsible parents who would rather run after a good time than care for their offspring. Often the grandparents step in and start child rearing all over again. I salute those of you who have shouldered that responsibility. God grant you wisdom and strength.

And He will. He gave Sarah strength to become a mother at ninety. He will give you strength to raise a child, whatever your age.

Participate.

The saddest thing I ever heard were the words of a friend's mother. Upon hearing that her daughter was pregnant, she said: "Don't expect me to babysit." *Why not?* I ask? We are not turtles who hatch our young and then swim off.

(It is turtles that do that, isn't it?) We are part of the cycle of life, and if we are part of the body of Christ, God expects us to support the next generation.

This is not to say that you have to do your children's job for them. Maybe your son or daughter is pursuing the "American dream": huge house, three-car garage with three cars in it, the latest in television, computers, cell phones—and the yearly vacation in Hawaii. If so, you don't need to support his or her habit by turning your house into Grandma's Day Care. (Unless you think that someone must be there for the kids—and that someone is Grandma. And you could have a valid point there.) But if your grandchildren's parents live modestly, try to serve God and raise a godly family, then certainly do all you can to help. Helping is the action that distinguishes a noble character. And the woman who says, "Don't expect me to babysit," needs to have her tongue taken away and not given back until she learns how to use it more wisely.

Many of us live too far away to be as actively involved with our children as we would like. For those of us separated by distance, thankfully we live in a high-tech age. Email, telephones, tape recorders and video cameras help us stay in touch. Grandmother Joan Treary has hooked up a video camera to her computer, which allows her to do conference calls. She is also a firm believer in sending goody boxes to the grandchildren at holidays. A box of stuffed bunnies and candy at Easter reminds children that they have grandparents who love them, and it certainly encourages them to associate Grandma with good things.

Joan also likes to mention shared experiences when she talks to her grandkids on the phone. On their last visit, the grandchildren enjoyed playing with her dogs. To keep those memories alive, she makes sure that they talk about the dogs in their phone conversations.

If you are skilled in crafts or sewing, make keepsakes for your grandchildren to treasure. I have one of my mother's delicate, handmade garters stored in my hope chest for the day that Honey decides to get married. If Grandma doesn't last that long, her granddaughter will have something special made with love for her by Grandma.

You don't have to make garters or embroider fancy pillowcases. A handmade sock puppet with button eyes can be a real treasure to a child. So can a drawing or a poem written especially for him or her. One grandmother I know enjoys sewing dresses for her granddaughters. I suspect those granddaughters take the beautiful dresses for granted. A day will come, though, when they realize how special those dresses were. They'll feel specially loved.

Psalm 127:3-5 tells us that children are a blessing from the Lord. That's true. And grandchildren are a double blessing. If you didn't appreciate your blessing the first time around, grandchildren give you a second chance.

Chapter 5

Social Insecurity

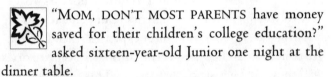

"MOM, DON'T MOST PARENTS have money saved for their children's college education?" asked sixteen-year-old Junior one night at the dinner table.

"Anyone for dessert?" I said quickly, even though Junior's words had made me lose my appetite.

But Junior has never been easily distracted, and he was still waiting for an answer.

"Yes," I admitted, "a lot of people do manage to save for their children's college education. Your parents don't happen to number in that rank." My husband had survived two lay-offs within five years, followed by a satisfying (but low-paying) job, and I felt we were doing well not to be sleeping in our car.

By middle age, most of us expect to be financially secure—with a nest egg saved for our future. After all, that's how our parents did it. (At least that's what I hear. My parents were self-employed and worked into their seventies because they didn't have the mythical nest egg.)

Today's job market and economy have changed since the '50s and '60s. There is no longer job security. Men today rarely work for the same company for forty years and then retire to putter in the garden. A typical man may, in fact, change or lose jobs several times before he reaches retirement.

People don't trust Social Security either. I hear comments like, "There won't even be Social Security by the time we're old" or, "The way health care in this country is going, who knows if we'll get the help we need?" Friends tell horror stories of fighting doctors to get needed treatment for their parents. Our generation's big questions are, "How will I meet expenses when I no longer collect a paycheck, especially if Social Security dries up?" and, "If I get sick, what then?" This boils down to one question: "How will I survive old age?"

My survey of women on financial issues raised a myriad of concerns. One woman said, "There's never enough money. Our three teens never stop eating." Another asked, "Who's going to take care of me when I'm old?" (Good question. We'll come back to it later.)

Our culture prescribes steps to financial security in our old age. But what if we have trouble following this prescription for financial security? And never mind the future. One woman said, "As a single parent, it's getting tougher to keep up with expenses." I heard from another single parent who was having trouble getting her former husband to kick in for college expenses.

One of the women I surveyed summed up my life when she said, "I feel the years are rushing by, and we have never been part of a company with a great retirement plan, nor can we ever seem to be able to save the recommended amount. I am afraid we will be rather poor seniors."

I agree. I'm afraid our financial portfolio would make an editor at *Money* laugh till she cried. (I know it has that effect on me.)

According to that highly favored yuppy magazine, it's not too late to get our financial houses in order. If you start at forty you can be a millionaire by the time you're sixty-five—if you have a household income of $84,000; if you put ten percent of your salary every year into a 401(k) plan; and if you're getting a typical fifty percent in matching funds from your employer and earn ten percent on your money.[1]

That's a lot of "ifs." The required salary knocked me right off the game board. All right, so I won't be a millionaire at sixty-five. I don't need to be a millionaire; I just need to be able to buy groceries and arthritis medicine. And thanks to a conversation I had with our friend, Mike—who, at thirty, is living off his investments—I think I'll be able to survive financially.

A while back, Mike told me that if my fifteen-year-old son saved just $7 a week for his life, he'd be a millionaire by the time he was sixty-five. I wondered about me. So I did some quick math. If I saved $7 a week for twenty years, I'd have $7,280. Figure in interest at eight percent, and I'd have $18,971. That's a long way from Millionaire Acres, but it's better than nothing.

Now, let's think about $7 a week in terms of investment and not just savings. If, at forty, I threw in a couple more bucks and saved $30 a month, and put it into a mutual fund with a fifteen percent return, (and didn't touch it), I'd have $100,000 by age sixty-five. Now I've got over five times what I had just in savings.

Most mutual funds require a monthly deposit of $50. That breaks down to $12.50 a week. Mike's mom, Penny, says that any woman worth her salt can save that. "You can save that much clipping coupons and not buying soda pop," she insists. I'm sure that even I could manage, somehow, to salvage $12.50 a week out of the grocery money. And I'll bet you can too.

You may be saying, "You'd lose that bet, Sheila." If that's the case, let's brainstorm a minute. What small thing could you do to get hold of $50 a month? If you are musical, giving just one music lesson each week would probably earn $40. Babysitting for a Bible study group once a week would probably net about the same. (Then you'd only have to lift $10 from the grocery fund!) If you have a sports skill, you can parlay that into private lessons. Tutoring is also a possibility.

Or you could get your investment seed money by playing some savings games. When you pay off an installment loan for a car, vacation or television, forget that you're finished and pay one more installment—this time to your savings. If your bill at the supermarket comes to $32.37, pay the checkout clerk $33 and put the difference in a special purse and funnel it into your savings.[2]

Another strategy: cut back a service you pay for and keep the money for yourself. Buy your newspaper at the newsstand instead of having it delivered; mow your own lawn. I'm giving up competitive tennis, and the bundle I save is going into a mutual fund.

"You can also put $2,000 a year into an IRA and deduct it on your taxes," says Mike.

"Wait a minute, Mike. I heard that IRAs are deferred, not deductible. There's a big difference between those two words, and getting them mixed up could land me in jail."

"No," he insists. "IRAs are deductible for most people. If your adjusted gross income is less than $40,000 a year, your IRA is always deductible. The next question: do you have a qualified retirement plan at work?"

"What's that?"

"That's an account where the company takes money out of your paycheck and puts it into a fund. You can find out if you've got one of these by looking at your W-2 form. There's a box on it that your employer will have checked 'yes' if you have a qualified retirement plan at work. If it's checked 'no,' it doesn't matter what your gross adjusted income is, and your IRA is deductible."

"All I can say to that is, amazing." (And that in itself is amazing, because I usually have lots to say!)

So, getting back to our mutual fund. If I feed that animal $50 a month for twenty-five years at a fifteen percent return, I will have about $165,000, one-sixth of $1 million! Now that should buy me quite a bit of arthritis medicine!

And the more diversified my investments, the better. Go ahead and invest in your company's stock programs, but companies can fail as the economy shifts. So remember: Don't put all your eggs in one basket, and spread your investment money around a little.

It behooves us all to take an interest in planning for our future because women will likely outlive their husbands for an average of twenty years. That will feel like forever to the poorly prepared widow.

You may be thinking, *But I've got to save for Junior's college education!* According to Mike, the forty-five-year-old woman who decides to wait until her son gets through college loses $75,000. "Is it worth that to wait five years?" he asks. Good point. Surely Junior won't miss $12.50 a week.

Which brings us to the subject of college. Some parents started saving for higher education when their children were babies. If you are one of these, all I can say is, "Wow! Truly amazing. You have been excellent stewards of God's money, and I congratulate you." If you are one of those wondering, *How on earth are we going to manage this?*—you are not alone. Many of us want to see our children launched into adulthood with as much help as possible. But we're a little worried about getting the boat out of dry dock.

For most of us, this issue works out one way or another. My brother and sister-in-law helped me by footing the bill for my first two quarters of college, and you may have a generous family member who would be willing to give your little Petunia such a start.

Since our Petunia didn't have a clue as to what she wanted to be, encouraging her to take a job (actually several) while she tried to figure out her future was more cost effective than shunting her off to college, where she had no desire to be. Now, she is starting community college. She earned every penny of the tuition money herself, and she and I are proud of that. I suspect that she will work hard to succeed because it was her own sweat and discipline that paid for the schooling.

It is amazing to me how God enables us to get an education in tailor-made ways. Some of my friends went to college on work scholarships or loans. Others paid as they went. When I began working as a waitress, my paychecks paid for tuition, and my tips took care of books, clothes and gas.

Now I see this generation getting scholarships or finding summer jobs that finance an entire year of schooling. One friend, Frieda Flounder, currently works in Alaska on a fishing boat, and she loves it. My friend, Patty Perfect, has a daughter following in her mother's successful shoes. The daughter received many awards upon graduation and a scholarship to the college of her choice. Barry Buff, our neighbor down the road, earned a partial football scholarship to a small college where he can pursue his career dreams in engineering.

Another young friend is moving to the big city to room with a friend. She'll attend a junior college for two years before she transfers to the more expensive university. My favorite college success tale involves my niece who got a college basketball scholarship. She embarrassed her three older brothers—all high school basketball stars who missed scholarships by a few inches.

And speaking of scholarships, there are companies who, for a fee, hunt down little-known scholarships. Check your high school counseling office for the contacts. Nearly 400,000 independent and private scholarship and grant sources are available in the U.S. More than eighty percent of these scholarships do not depend on family need or exceptional grades. They are based on factors such as the student's interests, hobbies, academic focus, age, heritage or parent's work or military service.[3]

I recently read of a $7.1 million grant in my state of Washington. The purpose is to beef up our state-sponsored Washington Service Corps and the federal AmeriCorps program.[4] Projects in this program range from tutoring at-risk children to delivering meals to homebound senior citizens. Students who take advantage of this program will get living allowances, health insurance and $4,725 in college vouchers after a year of service. The financial aid is out there; we just need to put out antennae to find it.

Each family is different, each child is different. I sometimes think that from our heavenly Father's view, we must present a fascinating kaleidoscope of lives; so many talents and dreams, so many of His children all going different directions. And He has equally as many unique ways of providing for us.

Knowing that He will provide for our needs, we can safely part with a portion of our income and give it for His use. Our friend, Tom, another excellent money manager, says, "Pay yourself first. Before you pay your bills, take a portion of your money right off the top and invest it."

Tom is close to right. I would say pay God first and yourself second. Since the days of Cain and Abel, God has requested we acknowledge His gift of life by giving Him the firstfruits of the harvest.[5] That principle didn't go out of style just because our culture changed from agrarian to industrial and then technological. Firstfruits, first profits—they both mean the same thing: honor

God and give Him His due before you dish out the goodies for yourself.

I think that principle applies to more than just paychecks. I think it applies to our priorities. Luke 12:31 tells us to seek God's kingdom first and the material things we need will be taken care of. His kingdom and His work should be our true vocation, and the place we work for our paycheck our witnessing field and our avocation. Wanting to please God should be our first and foremost goal. And when that is the case, we can enjoy true job satisfaction, and our needs are met. We may not get all we want, but we will get all we need.

I can think of two great examples of that. Thomas O. Chisholm wanted to be a minister, but due to poor health was able to do so only for a year. He wound up selling life insurance for a living, and he didn't make much money doing that. But God took care of him, and today Christians in churches all over the country still sing the hymn that is his testimony to the best insurance of all, God's care: "Great Is Thy Faithfulness."

I heard from a friend of an amazing widow named Louise Bourns who never had a lot of money. But that didn't stop her from giving large amounts to support her church's missionaries. Her friends told Louise she should save for her old age, but she felt called to invest in the present and future work of spreading the gospel. When her old age hit, a benefactor appeared who set her up in a retirement home for life. Talk about having your needs met!

If we are being wise in our spending and making God our number one life priority, He won't be so ungrateful as to let us starve. I believe that. So did the psalmist when he wrote, "I was young and now I am old, yet I have never seen the righteous forsaken or their children begging bread (Psalm 37:25).

I've seen this exampled in my own family, starting with my grandmother, who, in today's world, would be considered a little nobody. She stayed home and raised her family, and the last few years of that project she completed as a widow. As a grandmother, she gave away more of her years helping her son, who was left on his own, to raise his children. And when that job was accomplished, she came to us and was a second mother to my brothers and me. She never lacked for a place to live or people to love her. She also never stopped giving, and right up to the time she died at eighty-nine, she was doing the dishes and clumping downstairs in her granny shoes to the basement to do the laundry—not because my mother made her, but because she wanted to be a contributing part of the household.

My mother, now in her eighties, was a career mother. She devoted the first fifty years of her life to her children. Now she lives in a mobile home in the center of our family compound, the heartbeat of our little community. My oldest brother brings her lunch and dinner, my sister-in-law takes her on wild shopping sprees, my middle brother and his wife take her in to the big city for concerts and fancy dinners, and I take her to our ladies' Bible studies at church, run to the post office for her and have her over to play cards. When she's not socializing, she's busy writing letters to the editor and trying to save the country from moral decay.

I look at all this caregiving and see it as part of the circle of giving, God's amazing and touching survival plan for

His children living in a fallen world. First Timothy 5:3 is our guideline for caregiving. Paul instructs families to care for their elderly and, if there's no blood family to do that, then the church family is expected to pick up the slack. We are God's hands, helping those in need, and somewhere down the line, when we come to the place of need, someone else will reach out to us with His hands of love.

None of us can see what lies ahead. Some of us, in spite of all our planning and hard work, may lose our nest egg. If that should happen, our God is more than capable of providing for us.

That sounds like a pretty faith-filled statement and makes me sound like a regular spiritual giantess. Ha! When it comes to finances, my Achilles' heel, I'm usually more of a spiritual pygmy, and I often have to give myself the same pep talk I'm writing here. But the pep talk usually works, and the reason it does is because I've seen God provide for my family over and over again. He's proved Himself faithful in the past. He's with me in the present. Why should the future be any different?

Some of us worry more about the future of our health than our finances. The two biggest killers of women, cancer and heart disease, lurk in the shadows, and many of us live in fear that one of them may spring out and catch us as we totter toward the end of this life. Then there are health hazards like high blood pressure and diabetes.

We can't forsee every possible health problem lurking ahead on the road of life, but some we can anticipate and avoid. The woman who does body maintenance by exercising, eating healthful food and taking her vitamins is going to jog into old age in much better condition than her sister who opted to be sedentary and overdose on chocolate.

I must admit, I have had a hard time with this. Sugar has, until recently, been my drug of choice, and I often worried that my health would suffer down the road because of my addiction. Like the poor woman hooked on nicotine, I would think, *This is killing me*, even as I'd reach for that piece of cake for breakfast or dip into yet another chocolate bar. Recently a friend turned me on to a nutraceutical that dulled that craving, and I have concluded that my wild desire for sugar was an effort to fill a nutritional need in my body. Now that my diet is more nutritionally balanced, that problem seems to be coming under control, and I feel I have probably averted some serious future health problems.

If you are having a difficult time with aspects of your diet, you may want to meet with a nutritionist and do a little detective work. There may be an essential nutrient missing from your current food intake that drives you to eat the wrong things. Or, you could have a problem with emotional and spiritual roots. The Weigh Down Workshop is a diet program that deals with these issues, and which many women at our church have found helpful. (If you want further information about them, their web site address is: wdworkshop.com) Taking hold of our health issues now will stand us in good stead in the future.

Looking to your future, what do you see? Financial trouble? Bad health? Lack of mobility because of obesity? If the future is a place you don't want to go, it may be time to get yourself a road map. Road maps are wonderful things. They make a trip so much easier. With a road map there is no driving in circles, no stopping every few miles to ask directions, no arguing. We arrive at our destination relaxed and happy. I certainly want to arrive at my destination in that state of mind, so I'm going to follow two-lane superhighway SH (not state highway, but Sheila's highway) 62 into retirement. This road has two lanes: one is the fitness lane, the other the finance lane. To get on this highway, I have to do the following:

Plan

Health Plan

It won't do me any good just to say, "OK, tomorrow I'm going to exercise." Something will always come up to get in the way, especially if that exercise is not something I look forward to doing. The trick is to find something I like. For me, exercise is fun if it comes in the form of a game: volleyball, tennis, dancing, walking with a friend. I would rather die than miss a volleyball game or a tennis match with a friend, but going for a solitary walk? I can always find something better to do.

Analyze your personality. Are you a social exerciser, like me, or a solitary exerciser? If you are extremely social, find exercise that you can do with a team or another person. If you'd rather exercise alone, you might like biking or hiking, jogging or swimming.

Are you a jockette or a klutz? If you're not a natural athlete, you might want to pick something that doesn't threaten your self-esteem . . . or your neck. You might prefer walking to running, biking to softball.

Do you lack the self-discipline to walk alone? Get a friend to join you three times a week. Or pay for a membership in a fitness gym. I've found that I never miss doing something in which I've invested money.

Once you've discovered who you are, it will be much easier to find an exercise regime you can stick with.

After you've found what you want to do, make sure you write that exercise into your schedule. All my sports appointments are on my calendar so I won't miss them. If you are going walking three times a week, write it on the calendar, along with the time. You'll have a much higher chance of following through than if your exercise appointment is a vague "sometime tomorrow."

Vitamins are something I consistently forget to take. The only way I can remember them is to build them into my dinner menu—dinner being the one meal I don't miss—serving them along with the mashed potatoes. Making those extra vitamins a part of my diet now will pay off in health dividends twenty years down the road.

Financial Portfolio

My planning for my financial future is a lot like a farmer planning his crop. He knows he won't get any dividends until he's tilled, sowed, weeded, watered and waited. The same holds true for my financial crop. The money isn't just going to spring up in my checking account from nothing. I have to plant some money seeds.

Analyze your budget. Where are you going to make cuts so you can have the money to save or invest? Which paycheck are you going to dip into to start your IRA? Get information on the various mutual funds and decide on the one you want.

Take stock of your insurance situation. Financial expert Larry Burkett suggests that when planning for the future, we not only think in terms of savings but of insurance also. He suggests a supplemental health insurance plan even for those of us who have insurance costs paid for by our employers, citing the probability that, by the time we need it, Medicare won't be able to cover as many medical procedures as it has in the past.[6]

Finding a policy that will cover major expenses, such as hospital care, will help staunch the flow of money during that time later in life when we can't easily go out and earn more money to replace what we've lost.

Life insurance is another hedge against disaster. As I mentioned earlier, the chances are high that those of us who are married will outlive our husbands. Right now, my husband has a life insurance policy through his employer, but the time is coming when he will want to retire and we will need to consider getting a policy of our own, and for us, that means planning for that right now. We are going to have to budget some money for future insurance investment so I don't wind up living in my car.

There are many insurance companies, any one of which will be happy to take your money. To make sure you get a reliable company, you can contact an insurance company rating service.[7]

Gas Up

Most of us get gas in our car before we take a trip to make sure we will reach our destination. Stocking up on vitamins and tennies or a health club membership may be an expensive proposition, but those tools are the gas that will get you into your retirement years with a smile on your face. Saving money by doing without these things might cost you bundles in health care twenty years down the road.

In addition to fitness and health magazines, you might want to invest in periodicals that deal with money management. These are for you what the tractor and the fertilizer are for the farmer, the tools you need to ensure a good harvest of health and financial independence down the road.

Some people think this kind of planning shows a lack of faith. I disagree. Our heavenly Father will take care of us, but He expects us to take responsibility too. Living only in the present is a bad financial choice. Mr. Burkett says, "I wish that I could require every forty year old in America to counsel with a few retirees who have done the wrong things financially and are suffering with their consequences."[8] Proverbs 6:6-11 tells us to take a lesson from the ant. It "stores its provisions in summer and gathers its food at harvest." The ant looks ahead. So should we. And speaking of looking ahead . . .

Anticipate

"Half the fun is getting there," so the saying goes. Your journey toward your golden years can be fun. Exercise won't be painful if you have tailored it to fit your personality. Learning to eat healthy can be an adventure as you explore new recipes and new ways to modify old ones. And saving can be rewarding if you keep before you the image of a better future.

I'll admit, life might not seem half so much fun traveling in the finance lane if you are having to make sacrifices in the present to ensure a better future. You can make those sacrifices seem less sacrificial by occasionally rewarding yourself for your diligence. Before you get too excited, I'm not going to suggest you dip into savings and take a cruise. You can, however, have a party to celebrate after you've made your first investment in a mutual fund or opened a savings account. Once your savings has reached a certain level—$1,000, say—you can reward yourself and skip one deposit and use that money to go out to dinner. (That's *one* payment. Just *one*.) Even better, though, would be to find a way to reward yourself that won't interfere with your investment plan: rent a movie video, go roller skating, take a picnic to the lake, enjoy a bottle of sparkling cider in front of the fireplace.

Whether traveling by plane, train or automobile, there are times when the journey gets tedious. (Is there any one of us who hasn't heard the infamous question, "How much longer till we get there?") When taking a trip, anticipation carries us through the tedium of the journey. We think about what a great time we'll have once we arrive, and it helps us to hang in there. When struggling with a tight budget, remind yourself that you're struggling now so that you won't have to spend your golden years as a bag lady. That should help!

Some things we can't plan for. The years aren't always kind, and some of us may face heavy trials in our older years in spite of our use of vitamins and exercise. No one looks forward to the prospect of withering away or of losing our minds. I know I get a cold shiver up my spine every time I hear horror tales about older people suffering from Alzheimer's disease. *Not that, Lord,* I pray. *And not a slow, painful death, either, please. How about returning to earth before it's my time to die? That would be nice.*

Although we have no guarantee that we will be spared from crossing that dark threshold into eternity, we do have this guarantee that God will be there: "Yea, though I walk through the valley of the shadow of death, I will fear no evil, for thou art with me" (Psalm 23:4, KJV).

He really is with us, but not only *with* us, *in* us and caring for us. Jesus said that not even a little sparrow could fall to the ground without God's permission, and we're worth more to Him than the sparrows (see Matthew 10:28-30). He knows the way through the future and into eternity, and if we've put ourselves in His hands we can rest confidently that He will guide us. When I was a child, my mother taught me a Bible verse that has always stuck with me. It's Proverbs 3:6, and it says, "In all your ways acknowledge him, and he will make your paths straight." I believe that.

Survey participant Huguette Redinger, when questioned about grappling for a hold on a financially secure future, responded, "We are not dealing with these issues so much as the Lord is." And there is the bottom line. There may not be decent health care for our generation when we hit old age, and there may be no social security, but there will be God Security. Jesus said in Matthew 28:20, "I am with you always, to the very end of the age" —to the very end of our age.

And that's a promise we can count on.

Chapter 6

Midlife Crises Do Not Discriminate on the Basis of Sex

ONLY MEN HAVE MIDLIFE crises, right?

Right. And it's only coincidence that one normally strong woman in her late thirties suddenly couldn't cope with her children or her uncertain job status and spent her days crying or seeing a counselor. It's only coincidence that another woman in her late thirties suddenly discovered the men she worked with were infinitely more attractive than her husband. Another woman, a writer just turning forty, has spent much of the last year sleeping. She has had trouble completing projects and has exhibited classic symptoms of depression.

I don't think it's only the guys who hit middle age and suddenly find themselves in crisis. "Crisis" is not male or female. My dictionary defines "crisis" as a turning point, as well as the change in a disease which indicates recovery or death, as in *recover from this or die.* There's more than one way to die. We can walk around with beating hearts—but with numb minds and a nonexistent inner life. That is a much worse death than a mere physical one.

This halfway mark in life is the perfect time for panic. It is often the first time we've looked at the gas gauge and noticed that the needle has gone down overnight. We're suddenly mortal, with an hourglass half out of sand. Or we may see how few earning years remain, stack them against our financial obligations and realize that trouble lies ahead if we don't make changes.

Sometimes our crisis is like a deceptive hologram. It looks real, but it actually has no substance. That hologram can show us a failed life or a hopeless future. It can show us an impossible goal or a marriage too flawed to mend. When presented with a crisis, we need to touch that image with God's reality to see if it shimmers and disappears.

Assessing your life may cause you to think, *I blew it— my future is hopeless.* If that is the case let me offer words of encouragement, starting with Zephaniah 3:20. God warns the nation of Israel of impending doom brought on by their wicked behavior. But then He promises them a happy ending—even though they don't even remotely deserve it: "I will give you honor and praise among all the peoples of the earth when I restore your fortunes before your very eyes." He says this to a nation of idol worshipers.

Have you spent a good portion of your life worshiping the almighty dollar? Maybe you are up to your nostrils in credit card debt because you set your heart on fine things. God can help clean up your financial mess. He will rebuild your life into a testimony to Him. He will honor you—not with banquets, speeches and perks, maybe, but with something more lasting: the satisfaction of a good life and the love of others.

You may have worshiped at the shrine of good times. Maybe you spent the first half of your life rushing from one type of fun to another, leaving little impact on the souls of your family, neighborhood or world. You may want more said at your funeral than "We always called Suzie for a good time." It's not too late. For now, know that you can change yourself and the lives of others.

You may wonder what happened to the first half of your life. You were going to do great things, break the glass ceiling, become a success. But you are stuck in a job you hate and wondering where the time went. Maybe you just drifted through life and now find yourself stuck in a whirlpool, wondering how you'll get out.

My friend Bunny gave me a verse during a hard time. When things aren't going according to plan (my plan, that is), I take comfort from it like a worn blanket: " 'For I know the plans I have for you,' declares the LORD, 'plans to prosper you and not harm you, plans to give you hope and a future' " (Jeremiah 29:11).

If your past looks like a waste and your future looks hopeless, look to God. Ask Him to use all the talents, experiences, skills, heartbreaks and hope that make up you. God knows how to recycle and rebuild. He can lead you into new learning experiences, a new job or a new ministry—if you put up your antennae, listen to His voice and walk through the doors He opens.

Doors opened easily for me a few years ago when I published my first romance novel. I think those doors opened partly because I was moving. I had an idea for a good book and decided I had nothing to lose. So, with only a vague idea of what I was doing, I sat down and started scribbling. After a few months, I had a novel. Now what?

"Get a literary agent," suggested my friend Sharon.

Together, we perused Sharon's book of literary agents. "I've heard of her," said Sharon.

"I'll send her a letter," said I, and my writing career began. It started with an idea, but it happened because of action.

As a rule, doors don't open for someone who sits around singing, "I'll go where you want me to go, dear Lord." They open for one who proves she is willing by standing and walking out the door. It doesn't matter how noble the dream God puts in our hearts. If we aren't willing to move, He won't make it come true. It is as if an electronic eye in the dream door says, "Open and make way, she's coming through." If you feel trapped in a corridor full of closed doors, ask, "Are the doors closed because I'm not moving?"

One door has stayed not only shut to me but locked and bolted as well—even though I have banged my fists until they were bloody. That is the door of professional songwriting. (If I had all the money I spent trying to become a famous songwriter, I could have finished my house ten times over and gotten that new car I've harped about for years!) Looking back on my early attempts at songwriting, I realize that dream became an idol in my life. No wonder God didn't open that door for me. Once inside, I would have built a shrine to a false god.

If your dream hasn't come true, maybe you haven't gotten past the "sitting on the couch stage." Maybe you need to start going to school, searching the want ads, learning a new skill.

Maybe you have been chasing an idol that couldn't have brought you the true joy all of us, as God's children, need. Unachieved goals are sometimes just wrong targets. If you are currently in crisis, pray about that dream. Does it remain out of reach because you've spent years talking about it rather than moving toward it, or is it an idol? God will show you.

One survey participant confessed to feeling regret and sadness at this point in her life. She felt that it was too late for her to succeed. But I look at Bible heroes like Abraham, Sarah and Moses. Is it ever too late to let God work wonderful things in and through us? Life offers so much—hobbies, ways to serve God, adventures, new people, needs to meet, new skills and new dreams—that, even at midlife, we can still do, feel, think and be so much. There is no need to feel like you've missed the only boat in town. There are other boats leaving for many more locations.

Sometimes we haven't missed the boat at all. When I say this, I think of my friend Marion the librarian. She chose to put her career on hold and stay home with her two children. Marion always inspired me. Things ran smoothly at her house (as opposed to my house where things ran in all directions). Her considerable creative and organizational talents went into making a home for her family. She taught piano to supplement the family income and volunteered at her church. Meanwhile, her career languished on the back burner.

I recently visited Marion in her new home which was a step up from the modest tract home her family had lived in for twenty years. With her daughter married and her son on his own, Marion has finally gone back to work as a librarian. "I finally got my career," she said with a grin. After all those years, I'd forgotten she even wanted a career. But Marion hadn't, and neither had God.

God hasn't forgotten what it was you wanted to do when you were young and starry-eyed. With half our lives still before us, there is time. My friend Kathleen Hale says that with today's life span, the average woman can have three careers. I guess she would know; she's working on number two right now.

Midlife is when we often think, *Why did I marry so young? Why did I marry* him? One of my survey participants confided, "Sometimes I think it unrealistic to stay married for a lifetime to the same person when we change so much." (Underlying question: "Did I make the right choice?")

I would be willing to guess that this lady did make the right choice. But she's correct when she says we all change over the years. Individual change can, if we're not careful, gradually pull marriages apart until we suddenly face our mate from opposite sides of a wide, seemingly unbridgeable chasm. Suddenly, we have a marriage in crisis. After more than twenty years of marriage, I looked at how my husband and I were operating and suddenly realized I was not happy with the status quo.

We are the quintessential case of opposites attracting—and then driving each other crazy ever after. People

would often ask me, "How did you two ever get together?" Simply put, I thought he was adorable. Then I
realized he was smart. Lastly, I saw he was deeply spiritual. And he played tennis, my favorite sport (also the
only sport I knew how to play). What more could a girl
want? We got married. After the honeymoon, I realized
that one-half of us was extremely sanguine and a real
party animal. The other half was shy, hated big parties,
confusion and watching his friends break his furniture
when caught up in a wild parlor game. One wanted company all the time; the other wanted peace and quiet.
Could this marriage be saved?

Yes. I solved my problem by deciding I didn't need to
depend on my husband for my happiness. I could have a
great time with or without him. If he wasn't interested in
my latest passion, I'd leave him home. Alone. Just like he
wanted. That way everyone was happy. I discovered
roller-skating ("Man was not meant to be on wheels. I'll
fall down and break something," said my husband, so the
kids and I rolled on without him.) Then I took up volleyball. ("It hurts," said my husband, so he sat on the
sidelines while I played.)

Eventually, I was gone a lot, and my husband was no
longer happy. "You're never home," he would complain.

"Whose fault is that?" I'd reply. "You don't want to
do anything (that I want to do)."

Actually, I wasn't much happier than he was. After a
few years, attending functions alone got to be embarrassing; people began to think my husband was a figment
of my imagination. "We don't have anything in common
anymore," I lamented to my other half. "What are we going to do when we get old?"

Good question. But some of you may be saying, "Never mind when we get old. What are we going to do now?"

My friend Suzi Spalding was in that situation. Suzi preferred to talk rather than write down her thoughts to my survey, so I went to her office. I got to the last question, "If there is any issue related to the middle years you feel has been left unaddressed in this survey, please state what it is and what you think about it."

"Sex," said Suzi.

I blinked. This was the first respondent who had mentioned that word. "Sex?"

She nodded. "It's slowed down."

Definitely not a what-are-we-going-to-do-when-we're-old problem. "Whose fault is that?" I asked.

"Not mine," she said, and laughed. (I was relieved to see this was something she could laugh about.)

"So what seems to be the problem?" asked Doctor Sheila.

Suzi's husband, who is a teacher and coach, works twelve-hour days during the school year. During the week, he falls asleep on the couch by 8 p.m.

More of a night person and very social, Suzi didn't want to be left with only herself for company. She wanted attention, she wanted her husband to talk to her, she wanted intimacy. What to do?

"I didn't want to sit around twiddling my thumbs, but I wasn't going to opt for an affair," said Suzi, "so I joined the racquet club and played tennis in the evenings."

Talking further, we concluded that Suzi's need hadn't been simply physical. She craved intimacy with her husband, human contact, someone to pay attention to her. (All reasons why many women wind up in adulterous relationships.) Pouring herself into sports helped Suzi release a lot of sexual energy (I think the psychologists call that sublimation), and being with people took care of the longing for companionship. Her husband could doze on the couch during the week while Suzi enjoyed her friends and got a good physical workout. Then, when weekends came, Suzi and her husband gave each other their undivided attention. This arrangement made Suzi happy and took the pressure off her husband.

Now, back to my husband and me, the odd couple, and our looming golden years. We realized we would have to come up with some new interests to share or we would grow so far apart we'd never be able to bridge the gap. We already enjoyed travel, so that was something we could plan on doing together in the future.

But what about now, which housed a good amount of discontent on both sides? Well, we like the same movies and music, so now we're spending more time cuddling on the couch, watching old movies or Cliff Richard music videos. Tennis elbow and a bad knee have limited the amount of time my husband can spend on the tennis courts, but we've taken up ping pong, which is just tennis on a smaller scale. We indulge our love of music by getting together once a month with some of my husband's buddies to play guitars and sing, which makes both of us happy—my husband gets to pretend he's a musician, and I get a party.

To my survey participant who was watching the gap in her marriage widen, I can say I understand. At one point I looked at the gulf between my husband and me and wondered if my story would have a happy ending. I certainly didn't want to wind up like my best friend's mother. She lived in the same house with her husband but did everything alone because he wasn't interested in leaving his armchair. Facing the threat to our marriage and coming up with solutions we both could live with has ensured that, God willing, we'll share another twenty-five years together. Happily.

Well, happily until the next time one of us irritates the other. For all of us who have stepped into the harness with our opposite, it's best to remember how much we enjoy foods like sweet-and-sour pork. The unusual taste and texture combination makes it so interesting, and the differences between individuals make marriage a mix of comedy and drama. Opposites can drive each other nuts, yes, but they can complete each other too. We simply have to find a way to glue those two halves together.

Survey participant Jan Baxter sums up where most of us are when describing her relationship with her husband. She says, "Some days I could kill him, and other days I would just break his legs. But then he does something nice, and I'm nuts about him again." I think we all understand how you feel, Jan.

We all go through times when we question our marriage. And God probably has different answers. To some He may say, "This was your choice. You never consulted me, and that is why you are in the state you're in now. The only way it will improve is if you look to Me for guidance." To others He might answer, "I put you with this person because I knew he would jolt you out of your complacency." Or, "This man, although his temperament is vastly different from yours, complements you—learn how to make your differences work." Or even, "You are good for this person and being married to you will eventually teach him nobility and sacrifice." To my anonymous participant, He might say, "Seek my guidance. You can grow in your relationship and find new common interests."

Our society says, "Your needs are the most important. If the person you married doesn't agree with that, dump him. You'll be better off." I remember a friend who divorced his wife after a long marriage, saying, "The first twenty-five years weren't that great, and I don't want to spend the next twenty-five that way."

You may be thinking the same thing, but I encourage you to think twice. If you think you have a crisis now, wait until you start dealing with divorce issues: angry children, quarrels over assets, lawyer fees and confused married friends who aren't sure which one of you they keep and which one they don't see anymore.

Anyone finds relief in escaping a difficult situation, yes. But everyone will find enduring happiness by obeying God's will. Proverbs 5:15-18 sums up God's will for us as married people:

> Drink water from your own cistern,
>   running water from your own well.
> Should your springs overflow in the
>   streets,
>   your streams of water in the public
>   squares?
> Let them be yours alone,
>   never to be shared with strangers.
> May your fountain be blessed,

and may you rejoice in the wife of
   your youth.

There is something grandly romantic about a couple that has grown together and supported each other for a lifetime. Working through hard times is incredibly tough, but it can be done.

This advice may come too late for the woman who is already divorced and feeling guilt. God may be saying, "Accept my forgiveness." Daniel 9:9 tells us: "The LORD our God is merciful and forgiving, even though we have rebelled against him." You may have believed the lie that you would be better off without the husband you vowed to love and cherish "till death do us part." Perhaps you left because of abuse, or your husband said something like, "The first twenty-five years weren't so hot. I'm not sticking around for another twenty-five." If so, take heart. Isaiah 54:5 says: "For your Maker is your husband—the LORD Almighty is his name—the Holy One of Israel is your Redeemer." All who come to God may make that claim, including wives whose husbands walked.

A single woman may be raising clenched fists to heaven, demanding, "Why?"

God may say, "I have kept you alone because that is the only condition in which I know you'll turn to Me." Or, "You are unmarried because I want you to be concerned only with serving Me." Or, "I have called you to do great things which you can achieve only in your single state" (see 1 Corinthians 7:34).

He might say, "When you have accomplished everything I've set for you to do as a single person, then I will bring you a marriage partner." He might even say, "I brought you opportunities to marry, but you were too picky. Be more open to taking a mate who is flawed just as you are flawed."

Whatever has been spun from the choices we've made over careers or marriage, to have children or not, to reject or heed God's call—He can use these threads in the tapestry of our lives. Paul tells us in Romans 8:28 ". . . in all things God works for the good of those who love him." The Amplified Bible translates this as "all things . . . are [fitting into a plan] for good." Every one of us has a life that, by the time God is finished, will be a beautiful edifice. It will join an entire holy city standing for every other created being in every other galaxy to see with awe. But it's a long way from a blueprint to a beautiful building. Erecting that building involves a great many instruments of torture: saws, drills, nails, hammers, screws and screw drivers. Ugh.

Still, if I turn to God in my moment of crisis, search His word and pray, I'll reach my turning point. If I look to God, He will give me the strength to endure whatever misery I'm suffering. If I've taken a wrong turn, He will direct me to the door that leads to His plan for my life. How rough the journey and how deadly the destination when we take our own path! We find the deepest satisfaction only in laying our life before Him, following His impulses and going His direction.

Remember the hologram? Sometimes we create it ourselves by wrong perceptions of how our life should play out. When our expectations go unmet, it causes inner turmoil in our lives. Here are some possible expectations:

Now that my kids have moved out, I'll be free.

Not necessarily. You may barely get your offspring out of the nest before your mother swoops in for a crash landing. Or you may end up with grandchildren to raise.

I'll stay married until "death do us part."

Possibly, but you might also find yourself divorced or separated from a husband who has no desire to stay married.

I'll always have someone close by to love me.

I hope so. But your husband may leave or die, and your children may move across country.

I'm healthy now. There's no reason to believe I won't stay that way.

No reason other than statistics. You might have to cope with health problems for a season or even end your life battling cancer or another disease.

I'll find Mr. Right and get married.

There's nothing in the Bible that promises us that. God promises we will be loved and cared for, but not necessarily by an earthly husband.

I'll have children.

If this was an expectation you were hoping to fulfill, seeing the dream end along with the childbearing years is a bitter pill to swallow. Our culture doesn't solely place a woman's worth on her ability to have children. But it can still be painful when people ask, "And how many children do you have?" You see mothers snapping at their children in grocery stores and think, *Why her and not me, Lord? I'd have been a much better mother.*

I believe that God has a way for us to meet every crisis we encounter on life's road, and something for us to take away from it. I recently ran into an old college friend who reaffirmed that belief. In playing catch-up, I learned that Sharil and her husband had never had the children they wanted. "Yet one day, when I was feeling very sorry for myself," she says, "I realized that I have thousands of children."

She explained her prayers for a growing number of missionaries and new Christians around the world. She told me about phone solicitors who have called her and wound up finding a friend willing to pray about their problems.

The hologram of childlessness danced before this woman. It taunted and told her that her life was worthless. But in her moment of crisis, God showed her that her life is one of great service. When she gets to heaven, spiritual children will surround her. They will thank her for the prayers and encouragement that made such a difference in their lives.

Another friend reached a crisis point of dealing, once and for all, with her single state. She had three choices. She could sink to the depths of misery because Mr. Right hadn't come along. She could settle for anyone just to be married. Or she could make the most of her singleness. She chose the last. Today she's happy, successful and about to see her first book in print. She enjoys her freedom and her friends, and she's never had to change a diaper.

I think God allows times of crisis in our lives to shake us and wake us. Every time I get comfortable for a long spiritual nap, something brings me wide-eyed out of my stupor. My financial house of cards crumbles, robbing me of false security and forcing me to look to God. A child slides off the path of righteousness and has to be pulled back with prayer. Or a loved one dies, reminding me of my mortality.

I have been experiencing a writing crisis for the last three years which, I hope, will be over by the time this book comes out. After easily selling romance novels for several years, I listened to poor advice and fell out of the publishing loop. Then the book market tightened up, and suddenly I found myself out of a job. I wanted to continue writing in the secular market; we depended on that extra income. It wasn't right that, after all those years of easy publishing, I should encounter rejection. But encounter it I did, and the worst came when my literary agent dumped me. So much for my dreams of becoming a best-selling author. The YOU ARE HERE sign on my life map pointed to a deep valley. My husband tried to help by saying, "Look how far you've come." But how far I'd come meant nothing because I knew where I wanted to go, and I was nowhere near my destination. I was out of work, unemployed, laid off, rejected.

I got past the scream and shriek stage and asked God, "Why?" with a heart that really wanted to know the answer. And I eventually came to see His hand working for good in my misery. In the last three years I've improved my writing skills to compete in a tougher market. I have become more open to pursuing new paths and possibilities, which makes it easier for God to direct my life. This will probably lead to all kinds of new adventures.

Most importantly, I have come to realize that much of what motivated me to write in the past was pride and greed. That's probably the most important change God wanted to bring from my crisis. After all this analysis and work, I reached the turning point. I started to pull out of this hard time. If you are in the middle of a crisis, I suggest you too ask, "Why?"—the humble "why" of a child who seeks to please and wants direction. Only then can God lead us out of confusion and misery.

Our husband's midlife crisis can trigger our own. Many men reach a crisis point when they realize their life is half over. They have one pocket full of unmet goals and dreams and another pocket full of responsibilities that keep them from those goals and dreams. Your Dagwood may come home one day and say, "Guess what, Blondie! I bought a boat." Or he may pull into the drive behind the wheel of an expensive sports car. (Hopefully, he won't have a twenty-year-old woman in the seat next to him!) Or you may just find yourself living with a monster. In whatever form his misery erupts, I can guarantee it will make you miserable too.

You'll want to help. You can try a pep talk, but telling your husband to look at all he's accomplished probably won't get him through his crisis. He's temporarily blind, even with you pointing out the plain facts. I know this because I tried it. It didn't work. No surprise. It didn't work when my husband did the same favor for me during my writing crisis. But one thing did help, and I'll share our story in the hopes that it might help you.

Before we moved to our island paradise (translation: home still in progress), I noticed my husband becoming increasingly short-tempered and unpleasant. Even the kids asked, "What's wrong with Daddy?"

One night my husband and I talked about unachieved dreams. I'd been whining about my unmet goals which brought out his discontent. My husband is a planner, and his life had not gone according to plan. Here he was, entering his forties and still not doing what he longed to do: teach high school or college-level German. Coming up with the solution was easy: he would go back to school for his master's degree.

That wasn't so easy. It involved taking night classes, extending his lunch hour to take day classes and starting work early to make up for that extended lunchtime. Now, between going to school and working, my husband was beyond busy. But he was happier than he had been in some time.

Completing that arduous task was a real cause for celebration, but we soon learned that a master's degree wasn't enough. He needed more schooling, which would involve full-time commitment and more money. That was when we decided we needed to sell our house, leave the suburbs, turn our unfinished summer cabin into a real house (still not finished), and live happily ever after debt free so my husband could continue his education.

Moving to that cabin was the beginning of *my* midlife crisis. I can remember confiding to my mother-in-law, "I hate your son. I'm going to poison him"—not the sign of a happy camper. Moving hadn't been as easy as I thought. I had been uprooted from my home, lost my network of friends and my music activities. I knew no one in my new neighborhood—which consisted mainly of trees, anyway—and no one in this new community seemed interested in taking me under her wing.

But after a rough few months, we found a church and became involved. I joined the local PTO and the Welcome Wagon. I found people who liked to play tennis, and now I'm happy to announce that I am, once more, a happy camper. My cure came from realizing my discontent. When I understood that it stemmed from loneliness, I was able to get involved in the community, and the inconvenience of living in a house while building it wasn't so bad anymore.

My husband's life certainly didn't go according to plan after we moved. He wasn't able to continue on to get his doctorate. Corporate America wasn't kind to him either; he got laid off twice in five years. During that first period of unemployment we had a time where stress and tempers ran high, but we had a safety valve. Mine was my new network of friends. His was the house.

This house we're building was my husband's brainchild. He contributed to its design, wired and plumbed it himself, and even chose and lovingly laid the flooring. Watching it take shape under his hands was immensely satisfying for him. And a couple of years ago an opportunity came for him to teach German two evenings a week through a university's nearby satellite campus. He could never have done this if we hadn't moved.

Helping my husband make an old dream come true, as well as encouraging his new interest in home building, got us through the crisis. You may have a husband who is asking, "What have I accomplished? Where am I going?" Maybe a night of sharing dreams for the future (you go first to make it nonthreatening) will start a dialogue. Hopefully you won't have to move, like I did. But part of being there for the ones we love is the willingness to sacrifice. Seeing how well our life has turned out, I would go through all the misery again. Well, most of it.

It's not easy getting a man through a midlife crisis. You don't know what sort of crazy thing he's going to want to do. But taking steps to replant his frustration in positive soil will help your marriage, to say the least—if we can remain nonjudgmental.

Wait! Maybe I should define that word. Judgmental: having thoughts like, *What does he think he's doing?* Judgmental: saying helpful things like, "Are you nuts?" Or, "We're all going to die." And, "We can't even think of doing that." Nonjudgmental: realizing that it's important and natural to question your life's path, and that every human being does this at some time—including husbands.

OK, now we can continue. If we can remain nonjudgmental, we can help our husbands cope with their crisis and grow to be all God wants them to be. Now, is part of your midlife crisis asking, "What's my ministry, Lord?" Then I can tell you: Getting another person through his time of crisis can be a ministry in and of itself.

This is also the time of life when we begin to have more than a nodding acquaintance with the grim reaper, and facing him can bring us to a time of crisis.

Princess Diana's unexpected death in a car accident stunned the British and people around the world who loved her. One moment she was living and laughing; the next she was part of history. I'm sure that members of the royal family thought of things they wanted to have said or done differently. If only they had known she was going to die. If only.

One of my survey participants said, "Losing my parents has been much more difficult than I ever imagined. It has taken over a year to stop grieving their loss."

When someone close to us perches on the edge of death, we may wildly scramble to clasp his or her hand and pull them back. We may have trouble accepting a future without that person, or we may grieve over those things we wish we'd said or done. "You can't leave yet," we cry. "There's so much I meant to say, want to say, so many things I meant to do for you." Sometimes we get that chance, sometimes we don't.

Allow the grief to change you. Remember the famous Dickens character, Ebenezer Scrooge? Only when he saw death in the dark corners of the future did Scrooge understand the importance of life in the present. That close encounter with death changed his attitude toward other people. Death made him see what a short time we have together and how important it is to use that time well. We can't change the past. But we can use our grief to positively impact the lives of those who remain with us.

If you have a parent whose health is failing, Maudeen Wachsmith advises: "Don't feel embarrassed to make requests of God, and make them specific." Her family asked God to allow her father to live long enough to celebrate his fiftieth wedding anniversary. God kindly answered their prayers.

Maudeen says, "Ask." I would add, "Listen." My father spent his last days in the hospital the week before

Easter. My brothers and I and our families planned to spend Easter Sunday with Mom. My husband and I had decided to stop by and visit Dad on our way to be with Mom. But I felt the urge to visit him two days earlier, on Good Friday, as well. "You're going to see him on Sunday," reasoned my husband. "There's no need to make a special trip into town." So I bagged my rash plans. On Sunday we arrived at the hospital and found the door to my father's room closed. He had died shortly before our arrival. Then I knew that I had ignored the voice of God and missed my chance for a last loving contact with my father.

Listen to those promptings. Or you may lose the last chance to make things right, to receive one more smile or to usher the one you love to the gates of heaven. Even worse, you might miss the last opportunity to turn that one back from the gates of hell.

When our crisis is at its zenith, we may think, *I just want to run away, Lord.* That's what makes a crisis: God's heroine struggles in a blazing fire. Will she triumph and come out as gold, or will she yelp and run for water? My first choice is always water. God understands completely. The idea of going to an excruciating, undeserved death, of taking on humanity's sin and becoming repugnant to His heavenly Father, was so hard to Jesus. He even prayed before going to the cross, "May this cup be taken from me" (Matthew 26:39).

Yet He did go to the cross, saying, "Yet not as I will, but as you will" (26:39). By saying that, we too can overcome whatever crisis arises. Whatever your crisis, whatever half-finished state you are in, God has a plan. He will get you through your turning point if you just let go of the handle on that closed door. You may experience the death of a dream. But remember, after death comes resurrection.

When you face a crisis in your life, I suggest you sit with pencil and paper to answer the following questions:

What caused this?

Determining if your troubles are rooted in the physical, emotional or spiritual realm will be the first step toward survival. Are you in crisis because of faulty reasoning and poor choices? Or are you, like Job, going through a time of testing?

What spiritual lessons can I learn from this?

No matter what our situation, there is always a lesson to be learned.

What practical steps can I take to change this situation?

Most likely, you won't be able to answer this question until you have found the answer to the two before it. Once you have done that write down every idea that comes to mind—no matter how silly it seems. Somewhere, buried in those ideas, will lie your solution.

What can I do to survive spiritually and emotionally until my circumstances change?

Our circumstances don't often change overnight. Make a plan to survive and thrive until yours do.

No crisis lasts forever. It must, eventually, resolve for better or for worse, one way or the other. However your crisis is resolved, pray that it brings you closer to God and makes you stronger.

Chapter 7

Who's the Child?

I WAS HEADED TO Bible study with my favorite neighbor (who just happens to be my mom), and she was driving. Mom, who has shrunk over the years, sat on a pillow so she could see over the steering wheel. This made her just able to reach the gas pedal with her toes, which—incidentally—are full of lead. (I thought people were supposed to drive slowly when they got old, but I guess no one explained this to Mom.)

We had come down the hill to the highway and were going to make a left-hand turn at one of the rare traffic lights that doesn't have a green turning arrow. The light turned green. Mom started to crank the steering wheel and turn left—into the path of an oncoming truck.

Adrenaline shot out in all directions of my body, screaming, "We're all gonna die!"

"Not yet, Mom," I said, trying to stay calm.

She put on the brakes, let the nice man drive past, then tried again. Another car was coming. "Mom, we have to yield," I said, wondering if I was too young to start wearing Depends.

Mom obligingly braked, then repeated the whole process once more. I guess she figured that the third time's the charm. "Mom, wait!" I shrieked as a red car squeezed past us by half an inch.

The next car, probably fearing for his life, decided to turn left. So Mom cranked the wheel, stomped on the gas with her little lead toes, and we whipped through the signal. The adrenaline in my body returned to its cage, and my heart settled into a normal rhythm. I smiled sweetly at my mother and vowed to do all I could to end her driving days.

Driving is a sign of independence. No one likes to give it up, not even my sweet, tiny, eighty-something-year-old mother. But Mom is stoic. So, when my car died and my brother suggested she pass hers on to me, she said, "There comes a time. . . ." and surrendered her driving privileges. The fact that she could help her daughter who needed a car eased the transition to passenger. Now she rides shotgun with my brother or me when we run errands. We hit the card store, drugstore and grocery store. My sister-in-law, who is like a second daughter to Mom, delights in taking her to the shopping mall and encouraging her to buy wild outfits. And Mom, who still is able to live on her own, is content.

If this sounds idyllic, that's because it is. But not every parent is like mine. I've heard it said that as we age, our flaws become magnified—which means there is many a cranky, stubborn parent in Hometown, USA, driving their offspring crazy. Chances are, we'll not only fight the battle of independence with our teens, but with our parents.

One friend experienced a very rough year. She watched her mother, insistent on remaining independent, careen from one trouble to the next. After Mama nearly wrapped her car around a tree, daughter decided it was time Mother moved in with her. But Mother got cold feet, leaving her daughter wondering what scrape Mama would fall into next.

No one likes to admit she no longer functions well on her own. No one likes to admit that her body is crumbling or her mental capacities are slipping. And no child likes to see that happen to her parents. One of my survey participants talked candidly of how her mother's slow deterioration affected her. "I miss the fun we used to have," she says.

I still remember the first time I saw my mother limp. We were heading for a mother-daughter tea at her church. Mom looked adorable in her suit and high-heeled shoes, but she favored one leg.

"Mom, what's wrong?" I asked.

"Nothing, dear," she said. "My hip just hurts a little."

As the years passed, we went from "hurts a little" to hurts a lot.

"You've got to get hip replacement surgery," nagged her family and friends. One of her brothers really lit into her, and she got madder than I'd ever seen her. "I'm not going to, and that's that," she said. "Who would take care of Father?"

My father's health had never been the greatest. He'd battled a couple of serious problems and had emerged a hypochondriac. Mom was convinced that if she had hip surgery something awful would happen to Dad. And she would be incapacitated and unable to help him.

So she refused surgery and suffered restricted mobility. We used to walk together on the beach at our island home. Then she couldn't get down the stairs to the beach, and I walked alone.

Then came my father's death. He was such a part of all our lives. Granted, he often drove us all nuts. He freely dished out unsolicited advice. He always had a to-do list for his sons when they came to visit. But he adored his family. He was a high energy, life-of-the-party guy who taught his sons how to laugh and play jokes. Now he was only a memory.

Which brings me to another point made by a survey participant. One of the scariest things about watching our aging parents is this realization: they won't always be there. When our parents have been a big part of our life, it's hard to imagine life without them. Who will pitch in and watch the kids in an emergency? Who will advise me when I have problems with my husband or my children? Who will support me, pray for me? *Who will love me like my mother?* No one but the Lord. (And He'll love me even better.)

There comes a time when a mother relinquishes the role she has played for so many years. Her daughter moves from ingenue to bride, from bride to older woman. And then, one day, mother steps off the stage. Her daughter becomes the family matriarch. She becomes the support to *her* daughter, who naively believes her mom will always be there. . . until it comes time to take the baton from her mother's weak hands and run the distance allotted to her. That's the reality of life. The only way to emotionally survive this unexpectedly short cycle is to accept it and to make the most of the time we have with our parents.

My life gets busy. Although my mother lives next door, I'll go several days without doing anything with her. Then I'll think, *I may not have her much longer.* Now is the time to remember her. She wants my laughter now, not my tears at her funeral. She wants flowers in a vase, not on her grave. I stop what I'm doing and go next door for a visit.

One survey participant confessed, "I look at my mother and see the specter of me." We fear that we too will one day say foolish things and embarrass our children; that our memory will fail, and we'll grope for words that once rolled easily off our tongues; that we'll appear in public wearing tennie runners, drooping knee-high nylons and chartreuse shorts. Or maybe our fear runs to something more basic: the fear of death. We see our parents marching that direction and realize that we too are mortal. We are next in line.

I remember my grandmother sitting in the kitchen, deeply sighing and saying, "I just want to go home."

My mother, like all loving daughters who would rather not face the inevitable, said, "Mother, no you don't."

But Grandma did. Her body was wearing out. Her husband and dearest, oldest friends were dead, and she was feeling the call of paradise.

My thoughtful participant shared candidly, "I don't look forward to dying." As in *so why should Mom?* Frankly,

I don't look forward to dying either. I'm not afraid of my body losing function. But I am afraid of the pain I might go through in the transition into eternity. I do see, however, that most people reach a point in life where death looks less and less like an enemy.

The Apostle Paul wrote in Second Corinthians 5:4, "For while we are in this tent, we groan and are burdened, because we do not wish to be unclothed but to be clothed with our heavenly dwelling, so that what is mortal may be swallowed up by life." The first man and woman were meant to live forever in the bodies God created for them, but with their fall from grace came sin, disease and sorrow. After eighty or so years, coping with life in a fallen world gets wearing; we get tired of dragging around a rotting tent. If that body is racked with pain, the spirit longs to escape. There's no sting in death, no victory in the grave. The elderly person knows that. "We . . . would prefer to be away from the body and at home with the Lord" (5:8). She thinks about her worn-out body and says, "How can I lose? Take me, Lord."

Once upon a time, I chaperoned a junior high outing that if it wasn't from hell, it at least was attacked by it. We rode inner tubes down a river. A scary part of our adventure came when we got caught by nasty currents. We had already rescued one teenager who had fallen off her inner tube further back and were determined not to lose any more. I managed to get my three charges safely near the bank, but lost my inner tube in the process. It disappeared, leaving me clinging to the kids' giant inner tube. But the strong current pulled me away, and I went bobbing off at what felt like fifty miles an hour.

The water was cold, the current was fast, and I had no control over what was happening. My mind said, "Give in. You're going to drown. Relax and let it happen." My body said, "What a good idea!" Just as I went slack, our youth leader got to me and hauled me out.

The mental battle I experienced during my dunking in the river gave me a peek into my future. I know a time will come when, groaning under the weight of a fraying tent, my spirit will say, "Let go. You no longer need this; there is something better ahead."

I already have days when I just don't want to get up, and once up, hear protests from stiff and sore muscles. Some days it is too much trouble to fix my face and hair. (I never had a day like that when I was twenty!) If I have days like this when I'm middle-aged, how will I feel when I'm seventy-five or eighty?

No wonder so many old people sigh and say, "I just want to go home." Home means no more aches and pains, no more suffering, no more tears. Our elderly parents, so burdened with sickness and weak bodies, long to see their parents and mates once more. They long for home. It is hard for us who love them to hear them talk that way, but it's not unnatural for them to do so.

You might have a parent who is still perfectly happy with her tent; she is blithely unaware that her tent is unraveling. She may not remember how to boil water, but she insists on trying to live independently. She expects her children to keep her house in repair, mow her lawn and take her for a ride every Sunday. Or, like my friend, you could have a parent who excels at playing pin the fender on the tree.

If you are part of the "sandwich generation"—stuck between teenagers and aging parents—you probably find it difficult to help both ends of the sandwich. You may even consider running away. You wonder, *When do I get to rest?* You get to rest when you are no longer the sandwich meat, but a slice of bread. Meanwhile, try to build some personal health days into your schedule. Take an afternoon and go to a ball game with your husband. Hop in the car and hit some garage sales. Work out at the gym. Take a sauna, get a massage, do lunch with a friend.

In addition to getting away once in a while, get help. Set aside a quarterly work day when the extended family pitches in to help mom. This takes care of a lot of the painting and patching that needs to be done. Enlist the grandkids' help. Mowing the lawn once a week will teach unselfishness and the importance of caring for our elderly. It will also help keep a close relationship between grandparent and grandchild. If you live out of state, you may have to pay someone to take care of maintenance jobs.

You cannot shrug off a parent's needs, saying, "Someone will take care of Mom." *Someone is* supposed to take care of Mom, and that someone is you. God set this precedent when He told the nation of Israel in Exodus 20:12 to "honor your father and mother, so that you may live long in the land the LORD your God is giving to you." In Matthew 15:3-6, Jesus got after the religious leaders of the day. He bluntly pointed out their hypocrisy when they tried to wiggle out of caring for their aging parents. They said, "I'm afraid I can't spare money for you, folks. I'm already giving to the church" (the equivalent of "I gave at the office.") The Apostle Paul summed it up when he instructed Christians to put their religion into practice by caring for elderly members of their family (see 1 Timothy 5:4). This is how we pay back those who sacrificed for us. Just to make sure we get the point, he added, "If anyone does not provide for his relatives, and especially his immediate family, he has denied the faith and is worse than an unbeliever" (5:8).

You may be thinking, *My parents didn't sacrifice for me, I owe them nothing.* One of my survey participants wrote frankly of her neglectful parents, "They both deserve slow, painful deaths." Probably so. But caring for them anyway may be the most powerful witness of God's power that they will ever see. It demonstrates the love of God in a way words alone can never do.

Sometimes it would just be easier to make Mom move in with us. But we can't always do what is easiest for ourselves, because that might not be best for her. Mom will only go for that kind of arrangement if she feels needed. If she thinks you see her as another child who needs care, she'll die of malnutrition or a broken leg before she gives up her independence.

I have a friend who is determined to move her mother across the country to live with her. Mama's physical health isn't wonderful, and her bank account doesn't look too strong. But she resists all her daughter's well-meant attempts to transplant her. Why? Because Mama has a history and a network of friends where she lives. And although she might complain about finances, she doesn't want her daughter swooping into town and carrying her off. While Mama would appreciate financial help, she doesn't want her whole life tipped upside down.

Funny how that works. Every adult wants to be treated like an adult, no matter how needy she is. Managing this can become extremely challenging as our parents become more childlike and fearful.

Many of my survey participants talked about this issue. When her father needed a serious operation, one woman found her mother harder to deal with. During this time of crisis, her mother became discouraged and negative. The daughter tried to point out the rainbows in the dark clouds over Mama's head, which quickly became draining. Daughter coped by slipping away to take a solitary walk or a bike ride. Those spots of enjoyment helped recharge her batteries so she could return to her mother's side with a positive attitude.

One friend talked about arriving to take Mama to the airport. Mama was ready to go—along with several plastic bags of clothes.

"Those are my clothes for the trip," said Mama.

"Mom, you can't take things in a bag on an airplane. Where's your big suitcase?"

"I don't have a big suitcase."

"Yes, you do," said daughter. She found the suitcase and packed the clothes. Daughter also asked airline personnel to make sure Mama got to her destination. Good idea—because Mama took off in the wrong direction as she left the plane. Several frantic flight attendants chased her down and got her turned around.

One survey participant says she needs to be very specific with her mother. In the past, daughter and family came to visit "sometime in the afternoon." Now Mama wants to know exactly when. Another friend says that if she tells her mother about an outing too far in advance, Mama stews and frets over a million details. If Mama gets short notice, she has less time to worry herself sick.

To help you cope, here is a parent care survival plan to stick on your fridge:

Parent Care Survival Plan

1. When helping my parent gets stressful and I need someone to pray with me, I can call:

2. When I need an emotional break, I will:

3. These Scripture verses help me serve and honor my parent, even when I don't want to:

4. Phone numbers and information I need at my fingertips:

❧ ❧ ❧ ❧

When I volunteered in a nursing home, I saw many aged people who had been planted and then abandoned to thrive as best they could. When I think about them, I wonder if Galatians 6:7—"A man reaps what he sows"—applies to their children. The golden rule certainly does: "Do unto others as you would have them do you" (Luke 6:31). Would I want to be forgotten in my old age? Nope. Does my mother want to be ignored? Definitely not.

Remember, this too shall pass. You didn't remain a child forever. Neither will your mother and father—simply because they won't remain forever. Whether they live in a nursing home or your home, they want and need your respect, love and attention. Our parents cared for us; we can do no less for them. Even if their care was lacking, we still can do no less. Because in caring for others, we honor God.

Chapter 8

What Now, My Love?

 ONE OF THE WONDERFUL things about reaching the halfway mark in life is that you get a second blank slate on which to write. Well, it's probably more like a half-full slate if you're putting children through college or caring for elderly parents. Still, there comes a point when we have more free time than we once did. The kids have moved out, or at least they're not around much. The calendar is freer. The phone rings less. Things have slowed enough that we can take stock of our surroundings.

The map says, "You are here." Now, sit down, look around and figure out exactly where "here" is. Look at where you have been. Look at the paths that lie ahead.

(There are probably several.) The trick comes in picking the right one for you.

But it can be done. Proverbs 3:5-6 (KJV) says, "Trust in the LORD with all thine heart; and lean not unto thine own understanding. In all thy ways acknowledge him and he shall direct thy paths." Good advice. So before you put so much as a toe on any path, take a deep breath. Then pray, "Father, on which path would you like to see me set my foot?" He will show you. It's important to not roar down the first pansy-lined walk we find, because we can't see far enough to know what lies ahead. By seeking God's guidance we won't end up on a path that leads to a dead-end cliff. We won't end up camped on cement that will leave us spiritually starved. God specially landscapes paths with just the right amount of hills, valleys and beautiful vistas to enrich our life's journey.

You may be thinking, *Thanks a lot, God. So far Your path has only blistered my bottom when I've slipped and fallen. It's scorched me, rained on my parade and generally made me miserable. I'll pick the path for the second half of my life, thank you.*

You may have unknowingly picked much of the miserable route you've traveled your adult life. Much of the financial misery we suffer results from our poor money management, and health problems can arise from poor eating habits. Many relational problems spring from poor life skills, such as lack of communication or commitment, rashness and selfishness.

Of course, that's not always so. America, land of the free and the brave, is also land of the abused and the scarred. Some adults still carry gaping wounds acquired during childhood through no fault of their own. But those wounds can heal. If you are still bleeding internally when you reach the midpoint in your life, it's time to put yourself on God's operating table. Let him pull the bitterness, anger and unforgiveness from your heart.

We often cling to unforgiveness like a shield. *If I forgive this person,* we think, *I'll be vulnerable all over again.* But if you continue walking in unforgiveness, you are vulnerable to someone far more powerful than that person who hurt you. Satan himself wants to damage you for life and he will encourage you in your unforgiveness. Jesus has the true perspective on forgiveness. He said that if we—who are fallen and imperfect ourselves—don't forgive others, God won't forgive us. He can't.

In Matthew 18:21-35, we meet a man who owed ten thousand talents, an amount equal to about $10 million today. The man to whom he was indebted forgave his debt. But then he ran to someone who owed him a pittance and demanded payment. This behavior, when it got back to the king, didn't go over well.

God's point? Any wrong we do to one another is nothing compared to the magnitude of the offense when we sin against the One who made us all. God is willing to forgive us, but we must follow His example and forgive each other. His kingdom functions on the principle of forgiveness; unforgiveness gums up the works. The forces of darkness know it, which is why they work so hard to get us to hold on to offenses.

Unforgiveness festers the heart, making it sick and demanding. It causes us to focus on ourselves, making our souls small and petty instead of large and noble. This self-absorption is contrary to God's kingdom. Romans 12:10 tells us that the needs of others are to come first: "Be devoted to one another in brotherly love. Honor one another above yourselves."

Unforgiveness eats away at our peace of mind. One of my survey participants revealed that she and her father had never been close. "But before he died, I said everything I wanted to say to him," she says. "I forgave him for all the physical and emotional abuse. That gave me a deep sense of peace."

Releasing the death grip on the past is, indeed, freeing. We can't change the past, but by letting go of it we can change the future for the better. That's what my friend Betty[1] did. Betty's mother had been mistreated, and she had little to give her love-starved daughter. Betty's father was an abusive alcoholic who believed children existed solely to serve their parents. "Why else did we have all these kids?" he'd ask. Betty's mother wasn't around to answer the question. She was at work.

So Betty did Mom's cleaning and cooking. If Betty fell sick, she was on her own. She remembers one time suffering from two maladies at once. "Nobody should have to be alone with measles and bronchitis," she sobbed. No. But it happens when mommies don't ask God to fix their own broken hearts. Betty tells of when she asked, "Mommy, do you love me?"

"Go look in your closet," snapped her mother. A closet full of clothes and an empty heart; that was Betty.

The next twenty years weren't all roses, either. Although Betty did her best, her own children gave her grief. But before she turned forty, Betty forgave those who had wounded her and moved on. Now, at fifty, she's enjoying her grown children. As teenagers, they turned her hair completely gray. Now they are all strong Christians. She's teaching a Bible study and sharing what she's learned with younger women.

Two steps helped Betty leave her emotional baggage behind. First, she determined that she wanted to forgive and asked God to help her. Secondly, she looked at her parents in a new way. She saw her abusive father as a man who had, by rejecting God, made himself a pawn of the devil. It became much easier to forgive him.

I think Betty had something there. We are so much more than little ants scurrying around an ant hill. We are all created beings, living out a story far greater than any Greek or Roman myth. Enemies in an unseen realm continually challenge our allegiance to God's kingdom and His righteousness. Every one of our lives takes part in the cosmic conflict between good and evil.

Which brings us back full circle to the spot on the road that says, "You are here."

Where are you right now? Are you bogged down in a mudhole of unforgiveness? Whole books have been written on the subject. If this is something that has you trapped emotionally, you might want to discover one.[2] Study the Scripture and see for yourself what God our Father says about forgiveness.

You can't rewrite the script or rewind the video and retape what has already happened. But you can change direction. You can leave behind the bitterness and anger and set out on a new and higher path. This is the perfect time to do it, when you still have half a life left to spend.

Maybe you are looking back at the first half of your life, thinking FAILURE. If so, let's take a look at some first-half "failures" who went on to greatness.

One well-known man got off to a brilliant start. He was rescued from death as an infant and raised in a king's palace. But he blew his great beginnings when he settled an argument between two men by killing one of them. (That would end the argument once and for all). Our hero fled his cushy home and wound up living in the wilderness as a shepherd. That man was Moses, and God had to ignite a bush to light a fire under him and get him back into service. God speaking from the burning bush turned Moses' life around. He led the Israelite nation out of slavery in Egypt and into what is now Israel, the land God had promised to their forefather, Abraham.

Another of the Bible's heroes, Jacob, lived the first half of his life as a cheater and a swindler. His brother didn't take it kindly when Jacob tricked their father into giving him Esau's inheritance. Jacob had to flee for his life. But during his exile he truly met God, and his life changed.

Joseph, Jacob's baby son, was a spoiled braggart. God had great plans for him, and Joseph wasn't above mentioning that fact to his older brothers. They finally got tired of hearing how great he would be when he grew up and arranged to be rid of him. They sold him into slavery, and Joseph wound up in an Egyptian prison—not a very good beginning for a man who was supposed to become great. But Joseph learned humility in prison, and he did become great. By the time God was finished, the only man in Egypt with more power than Joseph was Pharaoh himself. Joseph used his high position to implement a food storage plan to save many people (including his own family) from famine.

Paul, writer of half of the New Testament, came to God with blood on his hands. He spent the first half of his life zealously perfecting himself. Trying to purge the Jewish nation of the fanatics who followed Jesus, Paul was responsible for the deaths of probably hundreds of Christians. That was the first half of his life. But look at how he made up for it in the second half. We owe much of our New Testament to him.

What have you always wanted to do—arrange flowers, write songs, start a catering business or become a fitness coach? Run for office? Congresswoman Carolyn McCarthy was middle-aged when she decided to run for Congress. The loss of her husband and wounding of her son in a tragic gun-related accident catapulted her into politics where she now serves as a congresswoman representing Long Island's Fourth Congressional District. She's living proof that a woman can do anything she's called to do.

Karen Christentze Dinesen, the author of *Out of Africa,* who wrote under the pen name Isak Dinesen, didn't see her first book published until she was forty-nine.

Are you inspired yet? Let me tell you another story about a woman named Anna Mary Robertson, who didn't have the leisure to develop her artistic talent as a youth or as a young housewife in Virginia. She expressed her artistic urges by decorating objects of daily use around the house and making pictures out of yarn. When her sister suggested that Anna try painting pictures, she did. Her son took some of her work to Thomas' Drugstore in Hoosick Falls, New York, where the art collector Louis Caldor saw them. And that was the beginning of the career of the eighty-year-old woman who would later be known as Grandma Moses.

One day I was returning from Seattle and struck up a conversation with a woman on the ferry. I learned she'd been speaking at a gardening convention. In fact, this lady was a celebrity in gardening circles, but she found this path after going through a deep valley.

At forty-four, Ann Lovejoy suddenly found herself with no husband. She had a life to remake and children to support. Total despair caused her to make a spiritual shift. "I felt forced into a corner," she says. "But if you're standing in a cornucopia, facing the narrow end, and you turn around and look out, there's no end in sight. I turned around; there was no one to stop me."

Ann's first step in her new life was to make a plan. She had a gift for gardening and had even written some books on the subject. She decided she could make a good living giving talks and visiting flower shows. The plan was huge, and at the time she wondered how she could make it all happen. So she went in stages. Now she advises, "Make a plan. It will happen."

Ann also suggests that, when assessing our gifts and skills, we try to look at ourselves with charitable eyes. We can easily see things that friends do well. "Mary, you're so good at planning parties. You'd make a great wedding consultant." We can do ourselves the same service. If you are having trouble seeing yourself with encouraging eyes, ask your best friend to give you some input. You might be surprised to learn just how talented you are. Like Ann, once you get turned around inside the cornucopia, you will be amazed at the possibilities the future holds.

The Bible is full of stories about new beginnings. But it also tells of people who started out great, then turned from God to live the second half of their lives in failure. Think of Solomon, the wisest man of the ancient world. He let his pagan wives draw him away from God, and wound up confused and disillusioned. Midlife is a time when we often stand at a crossroads. We can choose bitterness or discouragement, but we might not like where that choice takes us. We can choose to serve ourselves rather than God. But like Solomon we will wind up disillusioned. We can choose to shed the people in our lives who seem troublesome, but we'll still be left with half of the problem: ourselves.

The paths we take will determine whether we end up under a mudslide down the road or resting by a mountain stream. No matter what our circumstances, the high road is always calling us on to better things. Even if we wait until our lives are half over—hey, better late than never. Starting a hike at midday doesn't mean you can't still find beautiful scenery. We don't have to end up feeling like a failure.

I heard a speaker who was the ultimate example of how to make the second half of life better than the first. This woman had suffered horrible experiences in her youth. After her adoptive parents divorced, she went seeking her roots. She found them—but her birth father denied that she was his daughter. Even harder to accept was the suicide of her fiancé. In the race of life, this is not exactly what I would call getting off to a great start.

This woman may have fallen out of the starting gate, but she has hit her stride. She is coming into the home stretch with a life filled with good friends, poetry and her own business. She is brilliant and funny, and if she hadn't shared her sad past with 200 of us, we would never have guessed she ever had a care in the world.

So, where are you? You may be looking at your life map and saying, "This is no gold mine I'm sitting on. I want to be anywhere but here." The first half of your life may have been less than fulfilling. Maybe you got knocked off the corporate ladder and are still smarting from the fall. Maybe you never got a chance to even step on the bottom rung, and so you feel like you've missed out. Maybe, after years of waterproofing their lifeboats, you have launched your children on the sea of life. They no longer need you, and you are wondering what you are worth. Or perhaps, despite all your efforts, your children have not risen up to call you blessed like you read they would in Proverbs 31:28. God knows our wounds, and He can heal them.

He can also use past miseries to hurl us into useful and fulfilling service. I think of Barbara Johnson, a lady whose life didn't exactly flow smoothly. She lost two sons to death. Another became alienated and disappeared, and her husband suffered a devastating accident. When she was fifty, a publisher invited her to write a book about her experiences and how God brought her through them. Her book, *Where Does a Mother Go to Resign?* was the first of several best-sellers. For many of us, life does begin at fifty. Barbara Johnson is living proof.

Being a write-it-down type of person, here is my method for what to do when you reach a YOU ARE HERE point in life. Grab a pen and two pieces of paper. Separate page one into two columns. In the first column, list the hurts and wounds you are still lugging around.

That was probably about as much fun as a mammogram. But that's the examination part of the healing process. Now we go into surgery. Grab a concordance. If you don't have one, invest in one. They are the handiest things! Look up your particular illness in it. You may have to look under unforgiveness, anger, laziness or bitterness. If your life seems hopeless, look under hope, care or love to see what God has to say to you.

Whatever your problem, I can guarantee you'll find salve for the wound. Write the Scripture and what it means for you personally in the second column. If you are having trouble with this, call a friend or your pastor. That is what they are there for; that's what we are all there for.

As you work through these hurts one at a time, ask God to heal you. Ask Him to give you His view of your life and how He can turn the wounds you've gotten in this fallen world into something beautiful. We very rarely see the whole picture of our lives—just the painful red slash. But from God's perspective, we can see that red slash as a stroke in a beautiful painting.

The next page will be much more fun than what you did on page one—like going shopping for new clothes after surviving surgery. Consider it your reward.

Divide this page into four columns. In the far right column, write "dream come true." Under it, list your hopes and dreams. This could be anything from displaying your artwork in a gallery to becoming the first woman president.

In the left column, list your skills and talents. Do you sing like an angel, play a mean piano, paint pictures that leap off the page? Are you the fastest talker this side of the Pecos? Are you able to find fresh applications of Scripture to daily life situations? Are you a fabulous organizer? Write down everything you do well. If you are having trouble coming up with a list, ask your friends, your kids, your mother to name your skills. You might be amazed at all the things that end up in this column. Now, look again at that column on the far right. See any connection?

Move in to the second column from the left—and write "training/schooling." If you are just a bundle of raw talent, you may need to go back to school and learn how to harness that talent. You may want to explore career options or refresher courses. I heard of one woman who, because she was middle-aged and looking to train to reenter the job market, got a scholarship to her local junior college. My friend, Sylvia, is a master gardener and incredibly creative. She wrote on her midlife survey, "I wanted to oil paint for twenty years and I finally started." She is taking painting classes, and as she masters her new skill she's finding immense satisfaction in being able to at last fulfill a long-held dream.

You should have one remaining column to fill, the second column from the right. This is your "outlets" column, where you can list places you can contact after you've gotten your training or where you might be able to plug in right now. If you have good insights and high verbal skills, for example, you might write down working in a crisis counseling center in your column of possible outlets. If you're a fast talker, you might want to go into sales. Perhaps, like my friend Betty, you could lead a women's Bible study.

Your column might look like this:

Talents/ Skills	Training/ Schooling	Outlet	Dream Come True
• Creative • Good decorator	• Vocational school	• Re-decorate church bathroom • Help daughter wallpaper nursery	• Interior decorator

❧ ❧ ❧ ❧

If this all seems too complex and overwhelming, you can just sit down with a piece of paper and answer the question, "What do I see myself doing in five years?" Write down anything and everything that comes to mind, no matter how wild or crazy it may seem. After all, this is your second chance, your new beginning. You don't want to miss any exciting opportunity God might have waiting for you.

Whatever the one consuming passion is that you have denied, that one thing which, once upon a time, you were going to do, you can still do it. You may not make it to win an academy award if you've waited this long to become an actress, but then again you might, and you'll never know unless you try. And if you don't wind up with an Oscar, you can still experience the emotional high of acting in your church's Easter pageant or doing community theater. You may not give a piano recital at Carnegie Hall, but you can still take lessons and play for the sheer joy of making beautiful music. Like Isak Dinesen, you may be a writer whose time has not yet come. Maybe your time is right around the corner, and like Helen Hoover Santmyer, who wrote . . . *And Ladies of the Club,* your old age will be made sweet by seeing your great American novel published. (Helen was eighty-eight when her book became a best-seller.) You have the whole second half of your life left in which to do wonderful things.

You can start now. So far, all the lists you've made have been long-term. Now write down one thing you are going to make time to do, starting today, for God, for someone in need and for yourself. It may be as simple as getting up half an hour early for a special prayer time, writing a note of encouragement to a senior citizen or a Sunday school teacher in your church, and making an appointment for Friday night with a tub full of bubbles and a good book. Just making small changes will make you feel more like a rich and blessed woman than a harried, overworked and stressed out, unappreciated American female (which, incidentally, many of us feel like!).

My favorite fictional character, George Bailey from *It's a Wonderful Life,* is such a good example of what happens when we refuse to stop when God says, "Time for a coffee break." At several points in his life, George was given opportunities for enjoyment that he never took, and because he never took them, he turned himself into a human time bomb.

I've observed George Bailey's life for so many Christmases now that I can say his lines right along with him, and every year I yell at George, "Take a few days. Go to Florida with your friend. Here's your chance to get away, have an adventure!" He never listens to me. He doesn't listen when I tell him to scrape together fifty bucks and invest in his buddy's plastics factory, either. Instead, he struggles on, denying himself and taking no joy in the denial, no joy in the good he does, trying to single-handedly protect an entire town from mean old Mr. Potter, while deep beneath George's placid exterior resentment and frustration build until a crisis brings them blowing out of him like lava spewing from a volcano.

Don't be like George, confusing denying yourself with not being yourself. If a friend offers to send you to a writers' conference, go without guilt. Maybe God has a divine appointment waiting for you there. If your sister offers to pay your airfare to a family reunion, let her. (Remember that in allowing others to occasionally do kind deeds for us, we allow them to experience the thrill of giving.) If this is a time in your life when you can pursue personal development, do it; there is nothing wrong with developing our skills. And who knows how God might want to use those skills to benefit others further down the road? Laugh and cry and live life fully. Be open and ready for change. If you have been dying to take fencing lessons all your life, do it. If you've always wanted to punch a time clock and collect a regular paycheck, go try it. Let your light shine in the workplace. Take advantage of those talents God has given you and the opportunities He sends to develop them. And accept the treats in life with gratitude.

Don't think, like George, that in rejecting those little slices of fun that you are being noble. Rejecting opportunities for growth or turning our backs on simple pleasures is not being unselfish, it is being stupid. Eventually you will pay for your misplaced martyrdom when those feelings of resentment start to grow.

Even now, you might have talents that, if you started using them, would make you the richest woman in town and turn you into a member of that endangered species: a volunteer.

Why volunteer? If you were to ask Diane Blankenship that question, she would say that as women we are nurturers. "We don't stop being nurturers simply because our children are grown," says Diane. "Yes, we should continue to grow personally, but we grow in order to better serve others." Diane is right-on scripturally here. Jesus told his disciples in Mark 10:43 that "whoever would be great among you must be your servant" (RSV).

Diane points out that the temptation to self-focus is strongest when we don't have anything else on our mind. Diane has plenty on her mind. She is involved in Bible Study Fellowship, a parachurch organization that encourages in-depth study of the Bible. She also teaches Sunday school, and now that her children are beginning to leave the nest, she is making plans to start visiting residents of the nearby retirement home and reading to them.

Reading to little old ladies isn't your cup of tea? I'll bet you can find some avenue of service that will suit you. There's not an organization in America that isn't crying for volunteers. That's because we Americans value money more than anything else in the world. Our lives revolve around working, and usually we are not working for the sheer joy of seeing a job well done but so we can earn the money to indulge in enjoying our true love: buying. And with almost everyone off working for that second car, those fancy doo-dads for the house or that Caribbean cruise, there are very few left to give a healing touch to America's social ills. Jesus said that only by losing our lives to glorify Him do we really find them (Matthew 10:39). Discovering joy in serving others will add a dimension to your life that you won't find in any paycheck, promotion or award.

If you've equipped your children and watched them sail off into the sunset, you might want to expand your ministry to helping others whose boats aren't yet seaworthy. Maybe there is a teenage girl in your church who would love a second mom, one who appreciates her just as she is. My friend Betty has been that second mom for my daughter.

Honey is always welcome at Betty's house and loves to go up there and hang around Betty's kitchen. One afternoon I found my daughter there, up to her elbows in strawberries. She and Betty were making jam, something Honey had never done with me. What a great opportunity for my daughter to have such a mentor in her life!

Can you help some poor, struggling mother who is not getting through to her daughter? Probably. Simply by being there, by being friendly and showing interest, we can be a blessing in the life of a young girl. We can bring that girl into the community of women and make her see the specialness of her womanhood. Those of us who have been doing domestic things for so long sometimes take our skills for granted. We forget how overwhelming tasks like making jam or fudge, which seem so simple to us, may look to a younger woman. We forget how hard it was as a young wife to iron out the wrinkles in our marriages. Remember the Titus 2 woman, the one who instructs the younger women in godly living and good homemaking (2:3-5)? There is still a need for that, even in our modern world. Making yourself available to younger women can help meet that need.

Making fudge and jam and other domestic chores may not be your area of expertise. Maybe your strong suit is organization or people skills. Not to worry. The variety of volunteer options open to us is almost endless. The Red Cross, the American Cancer Society, your local school, your church would all love to see you coming with hands and a heart ready to work. You can help children who are having trouble learning to read, you can bake pies for a homeless shelter, you can run marathons and raise money for good causes. Whatever you enjoy doing, there is someone somewhere who would like to take advantage of your skills.

That someone may be as close as your own family. You may have children struggling even as a two-income family, trying to keep their heads above water financially and needing a parenting support system. Kids need someone to bake cookies with them, to take them to the lake and to take walks in the fall to collect fallen leaves. Maybe that someone is you.

All this talk about volunteerism may seem contradictory to what I said earlier. Enjoy myself? Serve others? Which am I supposed to do? Both. Life is not an either/or proposition. Life is laughter and tears, joy and sorrow, work and play. Read Leviticus 23:39-43 sometime and see the kind of party God could plan for His people. Jesus, our Lord, went to weddings and attended dinner parties. We work, we celebrate over a job well done. We serve God by serving His people, then we take time to enjoy those people and laugh with them. We give, we take. And we do it all, thanking God.

I once heard that on every piece of music he composed, Bach wrote, "For the glory of God." As I move into the second half of my life I'd like to be able to sign that same thing on every day of my life. Whatever new skills I learn, whatever new insights I gain, whatever new friends I make, oh Lord, let it be for the glory of God.

I hope that is your prayer too. Whatever the first half of your life was like, the second half still awaits you. Here is your new lease on life. Feel free to photocopy it, sign it, and post it someplace where you can look at it when you need inspiration.

NEW LEASE ON LIFE

I, _____ *(please print), hereby sign this new lease on life on this day* _____, *with the understanding that I stand at the corner of possibility and blessing, and before me stretches the road to growth and accomplishment. I commit to taking this journey toward eternity with Christ with eyes open to see new things and a mind and heart willing to experience them. I look forward to meeting new opportunities and making new friends, to discovering new ways to serve God and to finding a closer walk with Him. This is the beginning of the second half of my life and I sign this lease, ready to move into it.*

_____

(Your Signature)

Chapter 9

What Is Success?

IN AMERICA, SUCCESS MEANS the good life. If you are a mover and a shaker, you have the lifestyle to prove it: a big house with swimming pool and tennis court, expensive car, designer clothes. You will do important things with important people. We think of the Rockefellers or the Kennedys, astronauts, rock stars and Fortune 500 CEOs. We think of Dolly Parton, Oprah or Ivana Trump. Those who are more spiritual might point to Billy Graham or Kay Arthur. How many of us who live ordinary lives in average houses rank ourselves among the world's successful people?

One day I was talking with my beautician, my son and my mother. (How's that for an interesting combination!) I asked, "When I say 'successful,' what person comes to mind?"

My beautician answered, "Bill Gates."

Mom said, "Your father."

My son said, "Michael Jordan."

"Why?" I asked.

"Bill Gates is successful," said my beautician, "because he's intelligent, and he did something with that intelligence." Boy, did he! No one can deny that Mr. Microsoft is king of the computer world.

"Your father is someone who came up in a rough way. He's a self-made man," said my mother.

As I probed, she pointed out that he had done well as a grocer and had become respected in the community. Father had been well-liked, well-known, a founder of the local Lions club and active in his church. He'd invested in the lives of others. This was quite an accomplishment for a motherless boy who had dropped out of school.

I asked my son to explain what made Michael Jordan successful. Money and fame were the marks of success for my son, even though he qualified this with a less-than-complimentary statement about Mr. Jordan's character. Our hairdresser pointed out that Mr. Jordan had used his natural talent to get himself where he is today.

My son added our current pastor, Dan Samuelson, to the list of successful people.

"He expresses himself well," said my son. "He's well-educated." We all agreed that someone who is well-educated, who speaks and handles himself well in the public arena, is successful.

When I think of success, I think of good old George Bailey (yes, here he is again!), my all-time favorite movie character. George's real problem wasn't his lack of fulfilled dreams, it was his terrible affliction: blindness. He said he wanted to build things, but never saw that he was building a life of hope for the people in his community. He dreamed about being successful, not realizing that he already was. He couldn't see that he had, indeed, lived a wonderful life that positively affected many others. We're often just as blind as George. We say, "I'm not doing great things. (Translation: 'I'm not famous.') Therefore, I'm not accomplishing much with my life." Like old George, you may be impacting more people than you realize.

I have often talked with teachers who were amazed when students returned years later to thank them for their inspiration. I've seen youth leaders capture the hearts and minds of teenagers for God. I have known pastors who became second fathers to half the kids in their church.

It's not just influential people who affect others for good. My sister-in-law credits her best friend's family with introducing her to God by taking her to church with them when she was a child—a simple act with huge ramifications.

If your life looks like a failure, you may not be seeing the big picture. Maybe your definition of success is all wrong. Success isn't something we dress for or discover at seminars. Success is more than a large house, his and hers attache cases and kids with straight teeth. Success can be as big as winning the presidential election or as small as resisting the urge to stop for a hot fudge sundae. Success is seeing your offspring remember Mother's Day. Success is instilling a will to live in your house plants, getting up when the alarm goes off and mastering the art of shutting your mouth before your foot gets in it. It is the ability to enjoy a dinner out as much as a trip to Hawaii, and dinner at home as much as dinner out. Success is completing a trip without being separated from one you love—your luggage. Success is when you stop talking about what you are going to do and start doing it. It's making it through a day without losing your temper, a week without losing your car keys and a lifetime without losing a friend. Most of us are already more successful than we realize.

Success is about accomplishment but not necessarily fame. Let me tell you about some successful people I know. Betty Moorhead played the piano for worship at the church I attended for many years. She often lead the singing too. Some people might have thought of her as an ordinary schoolteacher, but those of us who experienced a church service with Betty at the piano never thought that. I have yet to see anyone as in tune with the Spirit of God as this woman when she lead our church in worship.

Barbara Hill would be the first to tell you that she is just an ordinary woman. I would be the first to disagree, because I know what she sacrificed. Like Abraham, she and her husband laid their son, Brad, on the altar and said, "He's yours, Lord." God said, "Thank you, I'll take him," and swept Brad and his wife off as missionaries to Africa. Then the grandchildren came, and Barb saw them when the kids were home on furlough. I can only imagine how hard those separations were on Barb. And God only knows how many people were added to His kingdom because she and her husband were heroic enough to give Him their most valuable treasure.

My sister-in-law, Marliss, never got her college degree or climbed the corporate ladder. Instead, she divided her time between raising five children and working as a custodian at the nearby grade school. Now her children are grown and have families of their own, but there is hardly a weekend that someone isn't home visiting. Over the years, Marliss has taken in foster children and run errands for elderly friends. She has met nearly everyone in her community and made an enemy of none. Her children and grandchildren adore her, and her community respects her. How many politicians could make that boast?

My other sister-in-law, Selma, remained unpolitically correct throughout her teaching career. She shared godly values with her students, exposing them to Scripture and traditional Christmas carols—while reminding her principal that the Bible is, after all, great literature. Who can argue with exposing children to great literature?

Jan Kragen, who teaches gifted children, not only has children dying to be in her classes, but parents as well. She has built a reputation for dedication and excellence, and her principal would do just about anything to keep her. Parents in need of counseling have come to her for advice on what to do with their children. When your principal adores you, your students are excited about coming to class and their parents and other adults clamor for you to teach them about history and science, I'd say that counts as success.

Jan's husband, Dave, lost his battle with ivory tower politics and failed to get his doctoral degree in philosophy. He's a househusband, using his spare time to write. He's still not published. Yes, Dave isn't much. He is only the stay-at-home parent for his daughter. He's only sponsored a refugee family from Vietnam and helped them survive culturally and economically in their new country. He helps build houses for Habitat for Humanity, works with an outreach to homosexuals, helps his friends design and build staircases and window seats, and volunteers with his daughter's youth group. What a failure is our Dave! We should all be such great failures.

Dave is in good company. Remember Jimmy Carter, the president who, in most people's opinion, wasn't much of a president? Like Dave, Mr. Carter has given his life to humanitarian causes. Why couldn't he be content to write his memoirs like so many other past presidents? Maybe it's because this man, who was elected to the highest office in America, defines success differently than the average American.

Sharon Gillenwater always wanted to be a writer. Finally, she worked up enough nerve to put down a story. It got published, and then two more after it. Another book won her an award. In spite of that, her career wasn't doing well. "No one wants to buy sweet romances," a literary agent told her. In other words, write some racy stuff, Sharon. Sharon couldn't do that, so she found an alternative in Christian fiction. Today, Sharon Gillenwater's books are found in Christian bookstores across the country. Right now, she has over a hundred letters piled on her desk from women who wrote how her stories have touched their lives. (That is more fan mail than she ever received working in the secular world!)

Speaking of books, every time I look at the gorgeous cover art on the dust jacket of my friend Candy Paull's first book, *The Art of Abundance*, I find myself grinning. I was one of many people who watched her struggle to incorporate beauty in a lifestyle based on a limited income. But she learned to find beauty in simple things. She has succeeded in life, and this book proves it.

My mother didn't start to drive until age fifty. Then my father, who thought he was dying, insisted she learn the real estate business too. But if you were to ask my mother about her biggest success, she would say it was raising her children to have a relationship through Christ with the living God. Her grandchildren too have placed their lives in God's hands. In this day, that is truly something to brag about.

Gene Berg is blind, at least that's what he says. But you'd never know it by the way he lives his life. Gene works full-time, repairs cars and plays a mean blues guitar. His wife will soon enjoy the house Gene built himself. He's done his share of building up God's people too. Right now he's part of the team at church who keeps our high-tech equipment working. He's not rich like Bill Gates or famous like Michael Jordan, but no one would label this man a failure.

Some of us are famous, like Joni Erickson Tada. She overcame extreme handicaps to inspire others that God can use us—no matter what our body's physical condition may be. But most of us may never appear on television or publish our life's story. Even so, we will still impact all who know us. Some of us are single, some are married, but most of us are more successful than we realize. Some are called to be singers like Amy Grant. Some of us are called to be singers like Betty Moorhead. Some may shine on the basketball court like Michael Jordan, others may shine from the sidelines. God doesn't care so much where we stand in life. It's what we do with what we are given that interests Him.

Matthew 25:14-30 tells of three servants whose master was leaving town. He gave each servant money to invest. One servant ably invested his large amount. The next servant had less, but he did OK. Servant number three got less than the other two. "My master's a slave driver," he grumbled. "If he thinks I'm going to be able to do anything with this change, he's nuts." The man dug a hole and buried the money.

Upon his return, the master praised and rewarded the two servants who invested their money. Then the boss turned to servant number three and said, "OK, Ralph. How did you do?" Ralph stuck out his chin and said, "You've never liked me. You hardly gave me anything, so what was the sense in trying to do something with it? Oh, don't worry, I didn't lose your precious money. I buried it to keep it safe."

If this servant expected a sympathetic reaction, he was sadly disappointed. "You turkey!" shouted the master. "You could have at least put my money in the bank and drawn interest." You don't need a lot of talent to accomplish something. (Half the singers we hear on the radio are proof of that!) God wants us to recognize and use our God-given gifts. The more we use those gifts, the more skilled we become. Just ask Simon Miller-Rhees.

Simon plays the keyboards on my church worship team. He first started with raw talent—very raw—but he loved the Lord, and he worked to improve his skills. Now, when I am gone, Simon ably fills my place at the piano bench.

Tim Heins spent the first half of his life as a drama professor. Now in his middle years, he's home with small children during the week while his wife works. On the weekends he works as a desk clerk. Tim's words are something for all of us to hold onto: "It's not so much what we do, as how we do it and that we do it with character."

True success is doing what God asks us with a humble and willing heart. It is thanking him for the talents He has given us—no matter how small—and putting them to His use.

Would you label yourself a successful woman? Ask yourself the following questions:

1. When I think about my relationships with family, friends and coworkers, do I smile or scowl?
2. Do I use the skills and talents God gave me for His glory?
3. If God said, "'You are going to die in ten minutes,' would I go willingly or beg for time to make things right in my life?
4. What will be said of me at my funeral?

If your answers to these questions trouble you, you might need to make some changes. Here is one more set of questions to help you get started:

1. What has been my biggest time waster, and what important things has it kept me from doing?
2. What do I want said about me at my funeral?

3. What changes do I need to make to ensure it gets said?
4. If I were to die tomorrow, what is the one thing I would regret not having done today?

Micah 6:8 says, "He has showed you, O man, what is good. And what does the LORD require of you? To act justly and to love mercy and to walk humbly with your God." That is the list of minimum requirements; I'd say that boils down to doing what we do with character.

Are you doing what you do with character? Are you taking whatever talents God has given you and serving Him with a loving heart? If not, what's to stop you from taking those first steps toward doing just that? After all, you still have half a life left. It is not too late to become successful.

Chapter 10

Parting Words

THE WOMEN WHO FILLED out my surveys had wonderful words of wisdom, so I thought I'd give them (and me) this last chapter for parting words of advice to all of you who are either in your middle years or about to enter them.

Physical Health and Fitness

This from an anonymous contributor: "Once your doctor starts you on hormones, stay in touch and let him know how you're feeling. Don't suffer in silence."

Hear, hear. If you start some form of hormone therapy, remember you are not the family dog. You can make decisions for yourself. You can speak up. You are the only person who will know if what the doctor prescribed isn't right for you, and—funny coincidence—you are the only person who can make sure the problem gets fixed.

"Find a female physician," advises Becky Gorton, "who will be understanding in listening and diagnosing and treating any changes in body and emotions."

Not every male doctor is heartless and insensitive. But I don't know any who have experienced PMS or hot flashes, either. If you feel your doctor isn't empathetic, find one who is.

"Stay physically active in something you like to do. Eat healthful meals and get rest. You don't have to keep up the pace you did in your twenties and thirties," says Doris Dungan. Doris also adds: "Do mentally stimulating things."

Our brain needs exercise just as much as the rest of us. I once heard that people who read, do puzzles and listen to classical music have more fit brains than those of us who become mentally lazy.

An anonymous contributor advises: "No matter what the cost, get your body moving and keep a positive attitude."

When coping with the more irritating symptoms of menopause, Jan Baxter says to remember, "This too shall pass." Good point, Jan.

Emotional and Psychological

"Talk to others your age," advises Carolyn Drinkwater. "Get into a support group. Tell your family what's going on."

I agree with Carolyn. If you are going through changes, don't think you'll be able to hide it. People will notice when you burst into tears because you just spilled the milk. And you won't be able to hide a hot flash on a November day unless you plan to walk around with a bag over your head. Life is about change. Admit it, accept it, share it. The sharing makes it all so much easier.

This from Doris Dungan: "Take and keep lots of photos. Keep diaries every year because as we age these will help us bring people and events back into focus."

This is something I wish I had done more. My first twenty-five years of married life are a blur. I would have liked to look at old journals or diaries. I don't imagine I will feel any less that way in another twenty-five years, so it would behoove me to mend my ways!

"Just take it nice and easy," says an anonymous survey participant. "Continue daily in the Lord's Word; find a great friend to share everything with."

Good idea. There is no sense fretting about what we're going through, whether it's hot flashes, trying teens or financial struggles. Jesus asks, in Matthew 6:27, "Will all your worries add a single moment to your life?" (TLB). The answer to that is simple: no. In fact, worrying is bound to do the opposite.

Another woman advises, "Concentrate on what is really important."

So, what is really important? I think the following advice from three of my survey participants tells us:

From Huguette Redinger: "Now is the time to get to know yourself and do those things (career, travel, hobbies) you could not do when the children were little."

From Denise Liles: "I hope that if I live to my eighties, or even to 100, that I will have a youthful mindset and enjoy life to the fullest."

And from an anonymous participant: "If you don't know the Lord Jesus Christ as your Savior, don't hesitate any longer. If you do know Him, get to know Him better."

This last piece of advice is so simple and, like breathing, so necessary. This is the age where we need to start thinking about getting our financial house in order. But even more importantly, we need to give our relationship with God top priority and give second priority to those people He has placed in our life. These investments will pay the greatest returns when we hit our golden years. If we haven't invested heavily in relationships, those years could turn out to be rock instead of gold.

Looking at the Positives

One of my survey participants complained, "I retain water like the Bonneville Dam!" Another, when asked what bothered her about her age, said, "The cellulite is awful!" Another woman hated "the way my body is falling downward."

It would be easy to look at our wrinkly necks, our widening bodies, our spidery veins and our jowly chins and think, *Lord, come before any more of me falls apart.* We may have a dead-end job, a stale marriage or, thanks to our children, be checking into the Heartbreak Hotel. There is probably not a woman reading this book who isn't dealing with some issue, large or small, that is related to this particular midpoint on the road of life.

But there are always problems lurking in the bushes. One minute you've wandered off to pick berries and the next you find yourself in a nest of angry bees. That's part of the adventure. It is also inevitable.

If you are currently covered in bee stings, you might need some salve, so here are some of the positives to remember about middle age.

1. *We have wised up.*

One survey participant confided, "People think I know a lot because my hair is gray." Funny she should notice that. Remember Proverbs 20:29? "The glory of young men is their strength, gray hair the splendor of the old." My survey participants all agreed that they are now wiser than they had been in their youth. Take that, Lady Clairol!

If we are all wiser, we will be able to find the resources to cope with whatever unpleasant circumstances appear in our life's journey. That's what being wise is all about.

2. *Menstrual periods are a thing of the past.*

Those of us who have come out the other side will tell you it is great. Plus, many find a sexual freedom we might not have felt in the days when the house was full, the wallet was empty and our first response to the word "pregnant" may not have been, "Yippee!"

3. *We can be comfortable in our own skins.*

"Being able to look back over twenty years and see the emotional and mental maturity in my life, I like myself better," says Denise Liles, who describes herself in her earlier years as "an angry young woman." Struggling with health problems, Denise had a lot to be angry about. But as she has matured, she's learned how to take responsibility for her own health. She has researched methods of treatment and has found a lifestyle that makes her disease manageable. Denise confesses that she has been disappointed over not having the great career she wanted. But, she says, "I have come to believe that if homemaking is the only career I ever have, I'm going to enjoy it as much as possible!"

Sylvia Carlton-Cordero says, "You're already 'over the hill,' so you can lighten up, do anything you want to do and not worry about it. People will think you're weird or over the hill, anyway. So who cares?" Not me, Sylvia.

4. *We can rejoice in new freedom.*

For Joyce Jacobsen, the positive side of middle age is "the contentment of knowing I've gone through the hard parts: the newlywed stage, babies, the teen years."

Many of my participants now enjoy finding themselves full circle and back to newlywed status. The towels left in the bathroom are once more "His" and "Hers." And those towels are actually hanging in the bathroom, not thrown in a heap on the floor.

For many of us, this is a time when the house stays cleaner longer, the grocery bill is lower and laundry doesn't have to be done so often. We regain control of the car, the television, the phone and our schedule.

5. *We have the chance to witness change and growth in those we love.*

Each age brings its unique wonders. In our youth, we enjoy bodies that seem able to go forever and faces free of lines. Life is a platter filled with possibilities set before us. It is a time of firsts: first job, first car, first home. Many of us experience the wonder of marriage and childbirth. Every day is filled with potential. Then middle age brings a whole new set of wonders. We watch children in our lives grow from boisterous kids with runny noses and scraped knees into handsome young people with shining eyes and big plans. We wonder at their amazing transition, and we enjoy talking to them as equals.

We set out to conquer new areas and build more memories for our old age. Then, when we are old, we experience the wonder of seeing the same, age-old play performed by our loved ones. This time we are not on stage but seated in the audience where we can appreciate the kaleidoscope of talents, temperaments and interests that have sprung from our gene pool. We remember the good things God has done for us. We shed tears and chuckle over memories.

I think Huguette Redinger summed up how most of us feel when she said, "I don't feel middle-aged."

Maybe that's because middle age is not a feeling. It is a spot on the road between the beginning and the end. From there we look back and learn and then look forward and hope.

My skin may have a lot in common with old underwear, but my life certainly doesn't. Old underwear, when it loses its elasticity, is good only for the rag bag. I'm still good for plenty, and the best is yet to come. I think the same is true for you, too. And so, I'll leave you with the words of Kathleen Norris:

"I have discovered that middle age is not a question of years. It is that moment in life when one realizes that one has exchanged, by a series of subtle shifts and substitutes, the vague and vaporous dreams of youth for the definite and tangible realization."

AMEN!

Endnotes

Chapter 1 - What Do My Skin and Old Underwear Have in Common?

1. Cover of *Redbook*, September 1994.
2. Cover of *Ladies' Home Journal*, October 1994.
3. Cover of *Good Housekeeping*, October 1995.
4. Cover of *Family Circle*, April 1996.
5. Edited by Robert S. Lazich, *The Market Share Reporter* (Detroit, MI: Gale Research, Inc., 1997), p. 141.
6. Leah and Rachel's lives are chronicled in Genesis 29-31, 35 and Genesis 49:29-33.
7. Dr. Anthony Campolo, *The Success Fantasy*, Victor Books, 1980.
8. S. Goodman Interview with Judith Martin, *Modern Maturity*, March-April 1996, Vol. 9.

Chapter 2 - When Hot Nights Have Nothing to Do with Romance

1. Paula Dranov, *Estrogen, Is It Right for You?* (New York: Simon and Schuster, 1993), pp. 57-58.
2. Susan Rako, MD, *The Hormone of Desire* (New York: Harmony Books, 1996), p. 97.
3. Sandra Coney, *The Menopause Industry* (Alameda, CA: Hunter House, 1994), p. 184.
4. Ibid, p. 196.
5. Ibid, p. 200.
6. Rako, *The Hormone of Desire*, pp. 97-98

7. Dranov, *Estrogen: Is It Right for You?*, p. 85.
8. Dr. Jonathan Wright and John Morgenthaler, *Natural Hormone Replacement* (Petaluma, CA: Smart Publications, 1997), p. 44.
9. Rako, *The Hormone of Desire*, p. 85.
10. Betty Friedan, *The Fountain of Age* (New York: Simon and Schuster, 1993), p. 474.
11. Betty Kamen, Ph.D., *Hormone Replacement Therapy, Yes or No?* (Norato, CA: Nutrition Encounter 1996), p. 73.
12. Wright and Morgenthaler, *Natural Hormone Replacement*, p. 110.
13. Kamen, *Hormone Replacement Therapy, Yes or No?*, pp. 161-166.
14. Ibid, pp. 167-173.
15. Ibid, pp. 82, 87, 139.
16. Ibid, p. 145.
17. Michele Meyer, "Walk This Way," *Better Homes and Gardens*, June 1997, p. 94.
18. Dranov, *Estrogen: Is It Right for You?*, p. 55.

Chapter 3 - Mother, May I?

1. Dr. Mary Manz, "My Church or Yours?," *Virtue* magazine, May/June 1997, p. 53.
2. Eli's story can be found in Second Samuel, chapters 2 and 4
3. Joyce K. Ellis, "Lord, Bring My Child Home," *Virtue Magazine*, May/June 1997, pp. 22-27.

Chapter 5 - Social Insecurity

1. Lani Luciano, "Smart Ways to Retire With One Million", *Money Magazine*, April 1997, pp. 88-95.
2. "I Can't Save Any Money: What Should I Do?," *Family Circle Magazine*, January, 1978.
3. "Students urged to check all sources for scholarship money", *Arlington Times*, pp. 5; 14-97.
4. P.I. Staff, *Seattle Post-Intelligencer*, Tuesday, July 22, 1997.
5. Larry Burkett, *Preparing for Retirement* (Chicago, IL: Moody Press, 1992), p. 100.

8. Ibid, p. 270.
9. Ibid, p. 64.

Chapter 7 - Who's the Child?

1. Pat Rushford's book, *Caring for Your Elderly Parents, the Help, Hope, Cope Book* (published by Fleming H. Revel) offers helpful insights and advice.

Chapter 8 - What Now, My Love?

1. No, Betty is not her real name!
2. One such book is *Restoration through Forgiveness*, available through Last Days Ministries, Box 40, Lindale, TX 75771-0040.